DOUGLAS JOHN HALL

is Professor of Christian Theology in the Faculty of Religious Studies of McGill University, Montreal, Canada. The village life he speaks of in the first part of this book centres in Innerkip, Ontario, and its nearby county town of Woodstock, where he attended business college for one year and applied his learnings in the office of the local daily newspaper for the next four. All the while his major interest was music, which took him in due course to the Royal Conservatory of Music in Toronto to study piano and composition. When his interest extended to Christian faith and theology he became a candidate for ministry in The United Church of Canada, took his arts degree at the University of Western Ontario and his three graduate degrees at Union Theological Seminary, New York. His intention had been one year of study there, but seven years with that distinguished mid-century faculty (Niebuhr, Terrien, Beker, Bennett, Scherer, Muilenburg, Tillich, *inter alios*) saw the young Canadian through the completion of his study programmes, involvement in advanced scholarly research, early teaching experiences, and marriage to fellow student Rhoda Catherine Palfrey. His doctoral dissertation, *The Suffering of the Church* (1963), sounded a major key in his academic career. The discernment demonstrated then underlies the mature realism and foundational hope set out in these pages. Along the way, Douglas Hall's ministry has included parish experience in the northern Ontario town of Blind River, inauguration of a church college in Waterloo, Ontario, and the McDougald Professorship of Systematic Theology in St. Andrew's College, Saskatoon. In 1975 he accepted the invitation to McGill and life in Montreal with Rhoda and their (now adult) four children. Lectureships have taken him to the two Germanies, Japan, and the United States. He is the author of numerous articles and some dozen books, including a major contextual theology in three volumes, the first of which is now available under the title *Thinking the Faith*.

THE
FUTURE
OF THE
CHURCH

Where are we headed?

THE
FUTURE
OF THE
CHURCH

Where are we headed?

DOUGLAS JOHN HALL

THE UNITED CHURCH PUBLISHING HOUSE

1989

Copyright © 1989 The United Church Publishing House
The United Church of Canada
ISBN 0-919000-57-6

Publisher: R.L. Naylor
Editor-In-Chief: Peter Gordon White
Cover & Book Designer: Robert G. Hoffmann
Printing By: WEBCOM Limited

Canadian Cataloguing in Publication Data

Hall, Douglas John, 1928 -
The Future of the Church

ISBN 0-919000-57-6

1. Church. 2. Christianity - 20th century,
3. Christianity - Canada. I. Title.

BV600.2.H34 1989   260 C89-093704-4

First Printing 1989
Second Printing 1991

For Gertie, Chuck, and Bob;
for St. Andrew's United Church in Blind River;
and for all the other 'exceptions,'
far too numerous to mention,
who have helped me to love the Church
in spite of . . . Christendom.

"He must increase, I must decrease"

– St. John 3:30

The humiliation of the church - the real humiliation - is that
we refuse to be humiliated.

– Albert H. van den Heuvel

CONTENTS

INTRODUCTION   - i -

I
WHERE HAVE WE BEEN?

Introduction   1
1   Christendom, Canadian Style   5
2   The Good and the Bad of It   10
3   'Something Happened'   16

II
HAS THE CHURCH A FUTURE?

Introduction   23
1   Responses to the Humiliation of the Church   24

    i   Denying It   24
    ii   Attempting to Recover Christendom   28
    iii   Behaving 'As If'   30
    iv   Seeking its Positive Meaning   33

2   Possibilities and Temptations for a Cruciform
    Body of Christ   38

    i   Authenticity   38
    ii   Orientation to Truth   39
    iii   Mission as Service   40
    iv   Self-Righteousness   41
    v   Mediocrity   43
    vi   Ghettoization   43

III
THEOLOGICAL DIRECTIVES FOR A DIASPORA CHURCH

Introduction: Beyond Christendom   49

1   Beyond Tolerance   56

2   Beyond Religious Simplism   59

3   Beyond the 'Issues'   64

Conclusion   67

IV
FACING THE FUTURE: TRUST AND IMAGINATION

Introduction: Ecclesiastical Future Shock   71

1   Christian Perspective on the Future   73

2   God is Faithful, We are Responsible   79

3   The Essentials   87

    i   Unity   89

    ii   Holiness   92

    iii   Catholicity   96

    iv   Apostolocity   99

Conclusion: On Wearing the Colours of the Court   104

INTRODUCTION

INTRODUCTION

"They want to finish it up," the old lady explained.

She was commenting on a meeting that she had just attended after the Sunday service in a downtown church in a large Canadian city. The congregational meeting had been called to decide upon a recommendation of the board of management. There had been an offer from a 'developer' who was ready to purchase the property, and it was evident that the managers were keen to go ahead with the thing.

But in the meantime opposition had set in from an unexpected quarter. During the past few years, the diminishing congregation of this old established church, once the locus of one of the most 'prominent pulpits' of the land, had been slightly augmented by persons unfamiliar with the aspirations of the solid white middle-class burghers whose 'church home' it had been for generations. Some of the newcomers were new Canadians, some of them black.

Learning in advance of the proposal that was afoot, a young Afro-Canadian had been inspired to muster support for a counter-proposal. He and his supporters felt that, despite its reduced and threatened state, the venerable church still had possibilities and should not be allowed to die.

It was on the edge of a large university campus, for one thing;

and while 'organized religion' seemed of little interest to contemporary students and faculty, profound religious and ethical questions were still (and perhaps newly) alive in the university. Just a week before, hundreds of young people had turned up in one of the university's largest amphitheatres to hear a debate on the subject, "Is There a God?" In the *post*-Modern era that we have entered, many who were shaped by Modernity have still not realized that "God" is not quite so "dead" as it was thought formerly! A society that has become secular *enough* to realize that unrelieved secularity may not be all that great manifests some astonishing new forms of "ultimate concern" (Tillich). At the end of her insightful novel, *The Ice Age*, British author Margaret Drabble, having followed the descent of her thoroughly secularized protagonist with great faithfulness to the realities of Margaret Thatcher's Britain, has him "find himself thinking" suddenly, "I do not know how man can do without God" -

> It was such an interesting concept that he stopped in the roadway, like Paul on the way to Damascus: not exactly felled by the realization, for alas, faith had not accompanied the concept. But it stopped him in his tracks, nevertheless. He stood there for a moment or two, and thought of all those who accept so readily the non-existence of God, who find such persuasive substitutes, such convincing alternative sanctions for their own efforts. Anthony had never been able to accept the humanist argument that man can behave well through his own manhood. Man clearly does not do so: that is that.[1]

God and 'all that' has made something of a comeback through the backdoor, 'Man' having meanwhile discovered a few of his ungodlike propensities. In universities, here and there, this discovery is intensive. So perhaps churches on the edges of universities ought to find out about that.

Besides, thought the resisting element of the congregation,

1 Harmondsworth: Penguin Books, 1977; p. 258.

was the church prepared simply to abandon the downtown core? Leave it to heaven, so to speak? Protestant churches had already all but forsaken the area - leaving the downtown *people*, the hurried people, the lost people, the hungry, sick, fearful and frustrated people of the City to their own devices. What had happened to the concept of the inner-city mission?, those who opposed the sale of the property wanted to know. Even if we don't have hundreds of people at every service and lots of money and brilliant leadership, they said, we still have space and - more important - we still have work to do here![2]

Surprisingly, perhaps temporarily, the proposal was significantly altered by this plea from the 'newcomers' - much to the consternation of some of the established families.

It was about the latter that the old lady - herself apparently one of them - was speaking when she said, "They want to finish it up." What she meant, I think, was something like this: 'Those of us who have been associated with this congregation for years and years, who knew it in its heyday, who heard its great preachers, yes and who paid its bills - we feel that it is our responsibility to bring it to a satisfactory end now. Endings should have some dignity, after all! And if it is left to these newcomers - well, there is no telling

---

[2] See in this connection the report of the Task Group on the Church in the Metropolitan Core, entitled, *A Dream That Is Not For The Drowsy: Urban Ministry for The United Church of Canada*, 1977. The following quotation is particularly apt here: "Many of today's church buildings face a multiple threat, and nowhere is the danger more evident than in the inner city where the rolls of long-established congregations are diminishing. At the same time, the costs of maintaining some church properties are causing congregations to go so far as to consider abandoning their buildings. Commercial developers, watching from the sidelines, tend to view this process of apparent decline as the perfect opportunity for purchasing prime land on which profitable apartment or office buildings can be raised. In the resulting climate of uncertainty, overtures by developing interests can be exceedingly tempting." [p. 14]. The Report warns, however, that ". . . we recognize the enormous social debt of each of our churches, incurred through the accumulated tax-exemption benefit: recognizing that the community has made a major contribution to the present market value of each property. For a church simply to sell out and take the proceeds for its private advantage would be irresponsible and unjust." [p. 31].

what sort of indignities will be visited upon this sacred place of our fathers and mothers. Certainly the newcomers don't have the money to keep it going. Besides, they have ideas that are . . . different. We don't want to witness the slow degradation and lingering death of these lovely and holy properties. Better bring it to a proper conclusion now, while we can still be in charge of the . . . last rites.'

* * * * * *

This is a book about the future of the church, and it is addressed particularly to those exceptional people in our midst who have concluded - *with their eyes wide open!* - that the church does have a future. I say "with their eyes wide open," because I suppose these reflections will seem strange and uncalled for by anyone who thinks that the future of the church is beyond question. It isn't. Nothing guarantees that the Christian church as we have experienced it in the West for sixteen odd centuries will continue, "world without end." On the contrary, it is pretty obvious to anyone who cares about the church's future that the vast changes which have been occurring in Christendom for nearly two centuries have accelerated since World War II, and that a great question-mark is written over the Christian future - not just the distant future, but the future that is already impinging on the present.

Both of the groups in the incident with which I have begun were and are aware of that question-mark. Both have the virtue of realism - and that, in the context of a North American culture-religion which goes in for a good deal of make-believe in this connection! - really is a virtue.

But there is (for Christians) a virtue that is greater than the virtue of realism, and that is the courage and imagination to entertain alternatives to what appears to be real, even inevitable. It is called hope. And only one of these two groups - significantly, the 'newcomers,' especially those 'new Canadians' who have known something of *great* deprivation and failure - exemplifies this greater virtue. May their tribe increase!

In the second chapter of this book I have described four types of response to the demise of 'Christendom.' But there is one response that I did not describe, because I do not consider that it warrants attention in a book of Christian theology - and that, despite the fact that it *may* be one of the most prevalent, if hidden, responses to this historic fact currently at work in and around the churches. I am referring to the attitude that seems to me, rhetorical disclaimers notwithstanding, to have informed the tactic of the managers (managers!) in the homely little parable above.

That attitude is: *Let it die.*

Behind this response to the humiliation of the church - a response which is rarely if ever stated outright! - there lies at best a sort of stoicism, but it is often just garden-variety cynicism. Its rationale may be something like this: The church has served a useful purpose, no doubt; and we shall honour its memory. But our pious forebears have gone and our children have lost interest, and we cannot account for the others, present and future, who may have some consolation out of these old stones. We ourselves shall be able to find our solace in other quarters, for the time being. Anyway, there will always be a place for us. But our duty, as the remnant of this once-proud institution, is to . . . finish it up.

I do not, of course, suggest that the closing of a church building is tantamount to giving up on "the one, holy, catholic, apostolic church." But in these *little* decisions, decisions about buildings and programs and ministries and the like, it is very often possible to glimpse, just beneath the surface, a very *large* decision about the Christian movement *in toto* - sometimes about the whole of life itself. It is not a pleasant thing to behold! Capitulation to death never is.

In the wonderful fable of "The Musicians of Bremen" by the Brothers Grimm, there is a refrain which is hardly ever translated imaginatively in the English versions. The old donkey, who first balks against fate and takes off for Bremen in search of something better, each time he encounters another animal destined to be summarily dispatched from this world, says: "*... Zieh lieber mit uns fort, wir gehen nach Bremen, etwas Besseres als den Tod findest Du überall....*"[3]-which means, roughly, "Instead of giving in to that, come along with us to Bremen; we can always find something better than death."

This, I suspect, is what a great many of us in the churches need to have brought home to us in these days. Again let me qualify that: I am speaking to and about those who know that death is real, and that the death of *Christendom*, too, is real. I have no wish to feed the sentiment that assumes an easy access to the future and ends in the shallowness of 'positive religion' and 'church growth' and other such gimmickry. The times call for sober realism about ... the ending. But they also beckon - and more pleadingly - to those who know that the best beginnings, *real* beginnings, always emerge at the point of real endings.

* * * * *

The core of this little study (I, II, and III) was offered as a

[3] Brüder Jakob u. Wilhelm Grimm, Kinder- und Hausmärchen (Stuttgart: Gustav Weise Verlag [no date assigned], p. 99.

series of three lectures to the Alumnae of Emmanuel College in Toronto in May, 1988. Some parts of these, in a revised form, were also given as lectures in the Lutheran Life Series at Waterloo Lutheran Seminary; and certain of the ideas that I developed on both of these occasions were first expounded in the 1988 Ebbutt Lecture, given at Mount Allison University in Sackville in March, and published as a monogram under the title, "The Future of Religion in Canada"[4] I am grateful to these three institutions for the opportunity to develop and share these meditations on the destiny of a movement about which I care deeply; and I express my thanks particularly to the Faculty of Emmanuel College for proposing their publication in some form.

Upon the invitation from Peter Gordon White of The United Church Publishing House to undertake such a project, I considered how best to render the material for print. In the end, I decided that I wanted to retain the 'immediacy' of the address form that belongs to the art of lecturing. At the same time, I was conscious of certain gaps and presuppositions that needed to be incorporated into a somewhat more permanent statement of these matters, and for that reason I added to the original three a longer fourth section (IV), written as an essay rather than an address. In the latter, I have attempted to speak to some of the questions, and include some of the valuable insights, that I received from persons who heard the lectures in one or another version. Part IV has also benefited from discussion with a group of students of the United Theological College in Montreal.

The "church" named in the title should be understood to mean the whole ecumenical Christian movement. At the same time, I have been particularly conscious of Protestant Christianity in the *Canadian* context, and, as the reader will soon recognize, there runs throughout a special concern for my own denomination, The

---

[4] Copyright © 1988 by Douglas J. Hall; available from the Department of Religious Studies, Mount Allison University, Sackville, N.B. E0A 3C0.

United Church of Canada, in whose present struggles it is possible for the discerning to detect birth pangs that will be felt by any church that tries seriously to make the transition from Christendom to that "new form of Christianity" which is "to be expected and prepared for," but cannot "yet be named."[5]

Faculty of Religious Studies
McGill University, Montreal
Winter, 1989.

[5] Paul Tillich, *The Protestant Era*, trans. by James Luther Adams (Chicago: The University of Chicago Press, 1948), p. xxii.

I

WHERE HAVE WE BEEN?

INTRODUCTION

Being by nature and inclination a rather introverted person, as I have found many Christian ministers and theologians to be, though we are oddly fitted out by seminaries and the sheer necessity of our offices for the performance of these public roles, I find myself somewhat overwhelmed by the general topic that I have been assigned for these lectures. To ask publicly about the future of the church - where are we headed? - is a fearsome undertaking! When I was somewhat younger, I was foolhardy enough to write about the subject on two or three occasions, and I suppose that is why I have been delegated to address you in these meetings - though many of you are undoubtedly more competent than I to speak about this, or more foolhardy!

Still, we must speak about it; because suddenly - yes, I think rather suddenly - we have come to the realization that the future we had anticipated, the future we had worked for and simply assumed, is not the future we are likely to get! As Arthur T. Clarke has said about post-Modern society at large (and it applies to the churches, too), "The future ain't what it used to be."[1] The rather overdone

---

[1] Quoted by Michael MacClear, Executive Producer of 'The Pursuit of Happiness,' in the CBC program, *The American Century*, Cineworld Inc., CBC 10/9/86.

response to Reginald Bibby's *Fragmented Gods*[2] within Canadian Protestant churches indicates that we Canadian churchfolk may have been a little late recognizing "the humiliation of the church," to use Albert van den Heuvel's nomenclature, since it has been going on for a couple of centuries; but now we too, for the most part, have come to the awareness that the future we had grown accustomed to expecting was simply not providing evidence of its imminent arrival. This has caused a minority amongst us to wonder whether our expectations were the right ones in the first place; others - and possibly the majority of those still associated with the former 'mainline' churches - are simply perplexed by this 'end of the constantinian era,'[3] and suffer ecclesiastical species of the "future shock" that has gripped large segments of the society as a whole.[4]

The first and most natural thing that happens to people confronted by an unexpected or shocking prospect is to grow retrospective. "Where are we headed?" quite understandably begets the companion question, the inquiry of this first lecture, "Where have we been?" Partly, this procedure betrays a psychic need to retreat from the anxiety of an uncharted future. Today the past, courted in various attempts to recreate or re-establish or refurbish it, functions as a lively temptation for many Christians on this continent. People are enticed into believing that the way into the future is through a return to some remembered past - usually a past more golden in the remembrance than it ever was in reality! Indeed, the main stratagem that seems to have been adopted by the majority of Christian bodies in North America, since few of us can any longer simply *ignore* time's quantitative and qualitative 'attack upon Christen-

---

[2] Reginald W. Bibby, *Fragmented Gods: The Poverty and Potential of Religion in Canada* (Toronto: Irwin Publishing, 1987).

[3] See Karl Barth, *How to Serve God in a Marxist Land* (New York: Association Press, 1959), p. 64.

[4] See Part IV for a further discussion of "future shock" as it relates to the churches.

dom,' is to try to reconstruct Christendom. I call it putting Humpty-Dumpty together again. The past and present are visited, often quite superficially, in order to discover how we might even now overcome the errors that are contained in them, and set to work afresh to achieve the majority status that fifteen hundred years of Christendom have conditioned us to call 'the Christian mission.' This in fact seems ultimately to be the object of Reginald Bibby's project: he spends a good deal of his book telling us what we have done and still do wrongly, and then he assures us that if we get it right - that is, if we can finally realize the universal demand for our gospel-product, and put our "fragmented" Humpty-Dumpty together again - we shall become the successful enterprises that we have awkwardly aspired to be.

There is another way of reflecting on the past, and that is to do so from a perspective that is consciously critical - critical, not in the sense of mere frustration and complaint, and not as a mood excluding appreciation, and not, certainly, as a covert way of blaming our forebears for the impasse we encounter today; but critical in the sense of wishing fervently to discern, from the vantage-point of the present problematic, the hidden and open assumptions and ambitions that have shaped us. Is the future that we were taught by our Christian past to expect and to work for commensurate with *either* the experienced present *or* the gospel as we are perhaps beginning to intuit it? Is it possible that our intuitions of a gospel appropriate to our present context are so uncertain, in part, because we are imprisoned in the Great Expectations or the silent and largely unexamined presuppositions of our Christendom past?

Clearly, any serious attempt to discern a future for the church has to come to terms with the church's past - and more especially with that aspect of the past which has to do with *its* way of envisaging its future. Where *have* we been?

There are numerous ways in which we might conduct such an

investigation. We could examine the pronouncements of church councils and committees. We could study the sermons of our Protestant past, the formal statements of theology, the liturgical and hymnological traditions. We could recollect the deeds and events of church history, perhaps especially the history of Christian missions. All these and many other aspects of the past would have to be considered if we were to answer in a full and responsible way the question of this first lecture: "Where Have We Been?" Moreover, all these things must be done, and to a certain extent have already been done, or at least begun, in many quarters, in our search for a way into the future.

But there are certain reasons why I would like, in this present statement, to take a different approach. What I intend to do here (and it is no doubt a risky thing) is to reflect aloud, with you, about my own past experience of the church. I do this for several reasons: first, I feel we should take the first person plural in this title quite seriously - Where have *we* been? It is too easy to turn this 'we' into something so impersonal and abstract (like 'the church' or 'Christianity' or even 'the Canadian churches') that it does not speak to the quite specific character of our own situation, past, present, or future. Secondly, while I shall presuppose, in what I say here, that you and I are more or less familiar with some of the scholarly work treating the church's past life and thought, it has frequently seemed to me that such work, precisely because it is 'scholarly,' is not quite rooted in the experience of 'church' as it comes to most of the people who actually *constitute* the churches. There is a temptation to read the reality of the church from the perspective of pronouncements in high places and the work and thought of gifted or prominent persons. If we are honest in our desire to know "where we have been," we must not judge this on the basis of where a few committees and policy-makers and delegates to General Council and teachers of theology and clergy have been.

And then there is another kind of reason why I have decided,

4

this time, to speak rather personally: This Spring, I have (to my own considerable astonishment) reached the age of 60; and it came to me as I thought about this assignment that The United Church of Canada and I are just about contemporaries. All but the first three years of our denomination's life are years that we two, The U.C.C. and I, have shared - and quite intimately at that! So I am going to draw on my own past, rather shamelessly, in order to answer the question, "Where have *we* been?" - though of course I want to do so as someone who brings to this biographical testimony certain preliminary and studied theological concerns, and so I shall be using my personal experience for what I hope is the larger purpose of illustrating a more expansive analysis of our ecclesiastical sojourn. I know that my experience of The United Church is not everyone's experience of it. Some of you - and especially those of you who were reared in large cities - *may* have to give quite different answers to the question posed in the title of this lecture. At the same time, I am bold enough to suspect that many people in The United Church of Canada, being like myself the products of rural, village, or small-town life, will be able to identify with this statement by making relatively few changes in the data, however differently they may want to interpret it.

There will be three parts in this brief address. In the first I will try to characterize our past by describing the church in the southwestern Ontario village in which I spent my childhood, adolescence and early adulthood; in the second, I will comment on what I would now regard as the positive and the negative aspects of this formative past; and in the third I will try to interpret the changed situation which came to be sometime between the end of World War II and 1960.

1.   CHRISTENDOM, CANADIAN STYLE

There were two churches in my village: United and Presbyterian. There was also an Anglican church building, typically the nicest building of them all; but it had long ago been boarded up. It exists in my memory as a symbol of the fact that the humiliation of Christendom began long before my birth. What happened at the time of the union in 1925 was that one family, the Blackstones, moved from the Presbyterian to the Methodist Church; the Methodist Church became The United Church of Canada; and everything continued as usual.

The United (*de facto* Methodist) Church had a strong reputation for moral propriety, whilst the Presbyterians were, some of them, reputed to be ... drinkers. The message communicated to us 'loud and clear' as children of the United Church congregation was that Drink was the surest way to damnation, the cardinal sin of an hamartiological hierarchy which included smoking, dancing, and playing cards. Every fourth Sunday in Sunday school was designated 'Temperance Sunday,' and on these occasions the Temperance Superintendent, brother of the General Superintendent, presented illustrated lectures on the evils of alcohol. These were supplemented by an annual elocution contest, sponsored by the W.C.T.U., in which even Presbyterians might participate. Several weeks prior to the actual contest, which was held in the school, the village expert on elocution, also an avid advocate of Total Abstinence, would set up shop in the teachers' room of the public school, and one after another the participants in this sort of Oxford County version of *die Meistersänger* would appear before the august lady to be coached in the recitation of his or her temperance poem or story, many of them tragic indeed. I personally hold two or three medals to attest to my enthusiasm for this sort of drama. We were regularly invited, in the Sunday School, to sign the pledge - a thing that my father forbade us six to do, much to our embarrassment, because it was generally 'done.'

Incidentally, sex, the favourite sin of a later age, was not discussed - though it was practiced in and around the village rather

6

liberally, and, I do believe, in all forms.

Everyone I knew in the environs of our village - and I knew them all, with the exception of a few reclusive country souls - was associated with the church. Except my father. This meant that everyone, nearly, was either Presbyterian or United, though we knew that a parent or grandparent of this or that friend was Anglican or perhaps Lutheran, and therefore "different." There were as well two or three families of Baptists, who were, nevertheless, accepted as Christians, being in every other respect conformists. A rather titillating scandal broke out at one point, when some of the more staunchly moral members of the community were reported to be attending meetings of the 'Holy Rollers' in the nearby county town; and we all amused ourselves with exaggerated tales of these righteous personages actually wading into the Thames and being dunked, or rolling about the floor, babbling incoherently. The incongruity was too much!

Roman Catholicism was, to us, a strange and foreign rumour of a thing. Only in my teens did I actually meet some Roman Catholics, when I went to collegiate in the City. I remember being quite surprised at their friendliness and fundamental decency; but we did not discuss their religion. The truth is, we were all WASPS in my village - until just before the War when some of the reputedly 'useless' sandy farms of the area were bought up cheaply by people with impossible eastern European names, and turned into little goldmines as tobacco farms. These people lived in their own transplanted worlds; they did not associate with the rest of us, though, despite our training in the ways of Temperance, we were glad enough to work for them during the tobacco season, since they paid well, and it was sometimes said in our living rooms that they were in fact quite nice people, all considered.

In other words, pluralism - as we have come to know it—was more or less confined to fantasy. Missionaries on furlough told us, sometimes, about lands which had not attained to our degree of enlightenment, and these reports were liturgically buttressed by some of the hymns or religious songs we sang -

> *Into a tent where a gypsy boy lay,*
> *Dying alone at the close of the day. . . .*
> *Tell it again, Tell it again,*
> *Salvation's sweet story repeat o'er and o'er . . .*

We also heard that there were a few Jews in the nearby county town, and, the stereotype being what it was (and is?), they were all reported to be sinfully rich, having made a mint in junk-dealing and other barely respectable occupations.

There were two basic centres of community life: the churches and the school, and they were not strictly separate, though a very fine line distinguished school concerts from church sponsored affairs, a line that was symbolized, until the war, by the singing of the National Anthem: in school, but never in church. With the patriotism inspired by the events of 1939, there was a general consensus that God and the King were rather close after all, and that the National Anthem (*not*, by the way, *O, Canada!*) should be sung in church as well.

The seasons were punctuated by recurring social and vaguely cultic events - from the strawberry festivals of Spring to the fowl suppers and oyster suppers and Christmas concerts and New Year's Eve 'Watch Night' services and crokinole parties of fall and winter. Young Peoples' - the YPU - was eagerly attended by all the teens and young adults; no-one had to coax or cajole us, because this was where romances usually began, and to this day I can tell you in some detail about the mysterious but predictable progress of the court-ships of persons now in their 70s and 80s, or long since gone to their reward. The courtships were public affairs, of course, leading not only to significant social events (the inevitable showers, the actual weddings and finally the chivarees that were important diversions in our routine), but also replenishing the village population, which otherwise would have remained stagnant, since few people from

8

'away' (as they still stay in eastern Canada) would ever have thought of moving to our village.

Church itself was, I think, not so important as Sunday School. In my village of precisely 307 inhabitants (by my own census, taken in or about 1940), more than a hundred appeared every Sunday morning for Sunday School - and this despite the fact that we had to share the available clientele with the Presbyterians!

Ministers came and went, sometimes leaving their mark, sometimes leaving us feeling nostalgic and deprived, but more often merely with a certain curiosity about who would next appear behind the pulpit. On the whole we respected them, even the Presbyterians; and, with one glorious exception, in my experience, they all understood very well the character and the boundaries of their place in the life of the community - though it was frequently rumoured amongst the more prominent laity that their wives did not. They visited us - the glorious exception even visited my Father! They took meals with us sometimes, or tea. They were kind, and fatherly in a rather formal way, and I think what most people liked best about them was the unique combination of dignity and humour that the best of them lent to our life. Whether or not they could preach well was not so important as whether they could perform tolerably as masters of ceremonies at talent festivals or the larger weddings and funerals. I don't think any of us noticed their theology. We assumed they were supposed to use certain formulae when they prayed, and we expected them to base their sermons on the Bible; but I think, looking back, that we assessed them as to the stripe of their religion more by their degree of openness to what we thought radical modes of behaviour, such as dancing and card-playing, and also of course on the question of whom they chose to associate with most. Only about the one - the aforementioned exception - do I have any recollection of a 'different' sort of message, or something. Yes, *message*, I think, is the right word. At least, he seemed to want to tell us something we hadn't heard. Or didn't want to. He didn't (as people said) "last long."

2.   THE GOOD AND THE BAD OF IT

Now before I move to more recent aspects of where we have been, I should like to comment briefly on this little scenario, in which I have tried, on the basis of personal experience, to draw a picture of a Christian past that still haunts me (I actually often dream about it). I suspect it haunts the church at large.

I used to believe that it was mostly bad, this past. Well, not exactly 'bad,' but somehow detrimental, confining. Like many small town individuals who have subsequently lived their lives in big cities, I know what Harvey Cox meant when he said that the city was liberating.[5] I am still not able to be romantic about that village past. Only people who grow up in cities, with too much loneliness, can be sentimental about life in little towns. With both Robertson Davies and Alice Monroe, who write about that same past, and with the late Margaret Laurence, I nurture a love-hate relationship with it. But the more perspective I gain on it - or, to put it in another way, the more I see of what has replaced it - the less prone I am to finding it altogether wanting. I feel about that past something like what Heinrich Böll felt about the previous century when he said, "Let us not condemn the 19th century until we have got through the 20th!"

There are many dimensions of that past that should be treasured: We knew, most of us, what it meant to *belong*. To belong to the school, to belong to the village, to belong to the church, to belong to the YPU, to belong to the choir - to belong! The word alienation was unknown to us - and so, except for the *deepest* manifestation of it, was the experience. We belonged.

Not only that, but we *participated*. Nobody spoke about

---

[5]   *The Secular City: Secularization and Urbanization in Theological Perspective* (New York: The MacMillan Company, 1965); Chapter 2, pp. 38 ff.

"Participaction" and we would not have understood all that, but we simply did it. We took our turns at being presidents and secretaries of little organizations, and leading in worship, and acting in plays and pantomimes and Christmas pageants ... and Temperance Nights. There were very few constitutional spectators amongst us; we were all participants. We actually *played* the games, we actually *sang* the songs. I have played the piano for church and community sing-songs for two or three hours running - and nobody had to have the words photocopied! We knew the words, and the music too. We participated.

We also imbibed what today would be called—strangely, significantly! - 'values.' We didn't know we were imbibing values, we just thought it was what you did. Or if you didn't do it, then you knew what it was you weren't doing!

Even about the church in that social setting (and I am going to say some critical things about the church in a moment - please be patient), one cannot in retrospect be *simply critical*. The church in my village was certainly a clearcut case of "culture religion," as Peter Berger and others have since detailed it. But at least it meant that the 'culture', so called, that is the general life of the village, was provided with some kind of cultus. I mean, think how dismal, how utterly flat and one-dimensional our WASPish communities would have been without some little reminiscence of eternity, some "rumour of angels," some outlet for the spiritual restlessness of heart that not even anglophone practicality can wholly extinguish! The churches of my village, back then, were not gothic cathedrals, and in fact they were so protestantly bright, both day and night (excepting for the CGIT candlelight service!) that it was rare for any ray of transcendence to enter! But sometimes there were moments of poignancy, when friendships and family ties would be unexpectedly hallowed by the quiet drone of the preacher's voice, or *some* voice, or when the rather mediocre poetry of the hymns would bring one to a visceral awareness of what one took for

11

granted -

We share each other's woes,
Each other's burdens bear;
And often for each other flows
The sympathizing tear.

No, it was not all bad. Not bad. . . .

But here the theologian in me warns me not to capitulate to nostalgia. And not only the theologian. Already the child and adolescent that I used to be knew that something was wrong, something missing. Sometimes I think that I became a theologian in order to answer, if possible, the dissatisfactions of the child, or at least to try and comprehend them. Be that as it may, I shall allow the theologian now - fifty odd years later - to tell the child that is not quite submerged in me what he has discovered about what was wrong, what missing.

First, there is the matter of the aforementioned culture-religion. 'Where we have been?', so far at least as I have been involved in it, is in a past, a decisive past, which made no appreciable distinction between Christ and culture, to use H. Richard Niebuhr's categories. To be sure, we eschewed the *de jure* establishments of the mother- and father-lands from which we came, and one of the great heroes of our own ecclesiastical tradition, Egerton Ryerson of blessed memory, was at pains to prevent such a thing. But what came to be, despite the glorious exceptions, was surely a *de facto* establishment - a cultural establishment - at least as effective as anything produced by the legal arrangements in our parental European societies, and far more enduring. What has been more "established" by way of religion, in Canada, than the church which announces in its own nomenclature its intention to be "of" Canada? There are intimations of the future that we have entertained in our very name, and in the motto we still proudly display - *ut omnes unum sint*. That motto, so *appropriate* biblically and ecumenically, has nonetheless only partially cloaked certain ambitions that are latently but thoroughly constantinian!

In my village, whose only substantial barrier to the total victory of 'the uniting church' was the stubbornness and concupiscence of some of its Calvinist element, there was absolutely no sense of incongruity between the Christian gospel and the 'values' of the community at large. The closest that we came to anything remotely "prophetic" was in the insistence of our church's leading lights that the village should be *more moral* than it apparently could manage, despite its own avowed intentions. And more moral meant, in an almost exclusive sense, personal morality; and personal morality meant, in an almost exclusive sense, refraining from various temptations which constituted strange obsessions for those who harangued us on them. Already the child in me wondered whether personal morality ought not to include doing something about the pride, the self-righteousness, the obvious lack of compassion demonstrated so consistently by the *most moral people*.

The child also had incipient notions of the *political* dimensions of Christian belief; for this child was, as it happened, the son of a socialist father, a union man. That was perhaps even more difficult, in my village, than being the son of a father who ... drank! I remember that a great lady once appeared in our midst, a great Canadian: Agnes McPhail. She addressed us school children, and as I listened to her I felt for the first time vindicated of mine enemies! From this first lady of Canadian politics I heard some things that I had heard at home for many years - and perhaps, too, from that one minister, that ... exception. But my sinful euphoria did not last long. I was Agnes McPhail's only champion in S.S. Number __, East _____ - and I lost, ingloriously, in the ensuing fist-fights on the schoolground.

Since then, I have of course heard of J.S. Woodsworth and Salem Bland and the others. But were they not also ... exceptions? The church that formed *my* early image of Christianity was not a church that swam against the stream. Whether politically, culturally, educationally, economically, in terms of gender roles and sexual orientations and all the rest, the church of my formative years gave every indication of supporting to the full the fundamental structures of society, namely, of the dominant culture.

Secondly, the theologian would like to explain to the child a still more complicated wrong. There was pain in my village - a good deal of pain, in fact. The Thirties were not so "dirty" as they were for my contemporaries in Saskatchewan, but they were dirty enough! Many were on relief, most of us ran up bills at the grocery stores. If you became really sick, so sick that you had to go to a doctor, you would likely have to spend the rest of your life paying the bill. Unemployment was a vast shadow in every family. How often did my father, a C.P.R. section man, come home and announce that he had been . . . "bumped." How often did my mother have to employ all her ingenuity to create some soup or stew - almost, like the Lord God, *ex nihilo*. And we were better off than many. I remember, long afterwards, reading a phrase from Gabrielle Roy's concluding paragraphs in *The Tin Flute*: "Salvation through war!"[6] And I understood it perfectly, for it was only the war that changed our prospects, economically, in my village, as in Mme. Roy's Montreal.

But the pain was not all economic. In a society that prized morality above all, rhetorically speaking, people were easily, regularly, compromised. Young girls became pregnant. Little boys were caught . . . 'playing with themselves.' There were ugly scenes between husbands and wives and lovers. Habitually, and almost by some perverse law of nature, lives were ruined by gossip. People also became sick on a shockingly regular basis. They died often. Occasionally they died by their own design. Even children died. There were epidemics of scarlet fever, infantile paralysis - there was pain. . .

---

[6] Translated by Hannah Josephson (Toronto/Montreal: McClelland and Stewart Limited, 1947), p. 268.

And the child wondered, Does *God* feel this pain? Did the sweet Jesus-amidst-the-flowers on my Sunday School paper, encircled by happy children, know about the long dilirium of that little girl, Jenny, whose funeral we attended in the Presbyterian church that Spring? Did He hear the awesome wail of great stout Rose when she had to say goodbye, finally, to the mortal remains of her crazy old Mother, the only companion of her life? Did God know the sort of hell that must have driven young Billy to drown himself the night before his wedding? And what would Jesus have done if he had overheard what the child heard that night getting off the train from the city, when a fine proud woman, the mother of his friend, turned to another fine proud woman like a hissing snake - "You bitch!" And the child knew, somehow, that there was this triangle . . .

There was pain, you see! And one might give God the benefit of the doubt and believe that God saw and heard the pain; but that would have been, mostly, *despite* what one heard about this God in church and Sunday School. Not that God and Jesus were presented to us as just remote and uncaring, certainly not. That may have been the Presbyterian God, but not ours! We were believers in the God who 'strangely warms' people's hearts. But those who were presumed closest to God and Jesus gave off the definite impression that the way to deal with the pain was to accept it, *in private*. "Take it to the Lord in prayer," but for goodness sake do not turn up in church looking as if you were at the end of your tether! You can sing about 'clinging to the old rugged cross,' so long as you keep a stiff upper lip whilst doing so! Probably most of the pain you have fallen heir to is in any case the consequence of your own bad management or . . . "the sins of the fathers". So learn from it, keep going, and . . .

> Ask the Saviour to help you,
> Comfort, strengthen and keep you,
> **He** is willing to aid you,
> **He** will carry you through.

And do try to keep all this to yourself!

By the way, we never observed Good Friday in my village.

3. 'SOMETHING HAPPENED'

Between 1945 and 1960 . . . something happened. Well, we could argue about the dates, I suppose; but I doubt that any of us who have been around as long as The United Church of Canada, or nearly, would want to dispute the thesis that something happened. Precisely *what* happened is still a matter of much speculation and concern amongst the wise ones of our society. But most of us who have lived it are at least aware of some of the consequences.

For instance, my village no longer exists. Or rather, it exists only in the memories of those who were part of it then, and we are becoming fewer. Of course, there is still a place that is called by that name. There are still some of the old houses, looking for the most part rather dowdy compared with the landscaped homes of the new 'subdivisions.' The general stores and butcher shop have been transformed into 'craft shops.' People buy their groceries in the big shopping malls on the way home from work in the city; for my village has become, virtually, a 'bedroom community.' The two church buildings remain, much 'improved' and upgraded to conform, I suppose, with the tastes of those who inhabit the landscaped homes. The United Church now has a centre aisle and a chancel and a dorsal cloth and a very nice cross.

I do not know what happens in that church from Sunday to Sunday, year to year; I have long since made my home in the cities. But we all know what has occurred in thousands of communities like this all over North America. Modern industry locates in larger centres. The work is there and that is where the people go. If they do not go there to live, they go there in their cars daily, from their bedroom communities. Contemporary modes of communication

16

have produced a nation of spectators. Who needs oyster suppers and temperance nights when you can watch *Dallas* or put the latest Hollywood violence into your VCR? Contemporary transportation, aided and abetted by the fictions of the image-makers and travel agencies, spirits us off to far-away places, to Florida, to Hawaii, to Cuba: magic places for Canadians, for we are a wintertime people with summertime fantasies. The entertainment industry makes our funny little variety shows and our plays and church-shed festivals of yesteryear seem corny in the extreme.

In short, the centre has shifted - dramatically. The disappearance of community life has entailed the disappearance, also, of the the church as centre. We are speaking about the demise of Christendom, Canadian style. Christendom did not end here with a bang, as it did in eastern Europe, but with a whimper. So soft a whimper that most people didn't even notice. Besides, there are still full churches here and there - and there is still some money available. So it is possible to overlook the humiliation of the church still, if you are not very knowledgeable about what churches once meant for the life of little villages and towns, or for nations and empires.

But those who know what they once meant are still haunted by that past, and the truth is, I think, that whatever visions for the future of the church are operative in our midst today have been gleaned, for the most part, from the ruins of that past. The village church! - it is the dream church of every suburbia I know. No wonder that so many of our churches are full of an unrequited nostalgia. For we cannot really reproduce those small-town Sunday mornings that Norman Rockwell and the others imaged for us; they simply do not come off in the consumer society.

Well, the nostalgia is understandable. Some things have been lost - lost irretrievably, perhaps. It is well for us to admit these "intimations of deprivation" (George Grant). For all their immaculately bourgeois splendor, their coffee hours and dorsal cloths and suspended crosses, the suburban churches that replaced - whilst

17

trying vainly to imitate - the village church cannot provide the sense of belonging, of participation, of unselfconscious living that was part of all that.

But the purpose of my exercise in reminiscence was not to reinforce nostalgia. It was to liberate. We should let ourselves be emancipated from that past - that Christendom à la Canadian Protestantism! There was much that was good, true and beautiful in it; but there was also much that was just wrong . . . unfaithful . . . even demonic! We are too enthralled, still, by these dreams. We forget too easily how confining was that mode of the religious life, how consistently it prevented the gospel from being heard, how insidiously it identified the morality of bookkeepers with the new law of the Christ.

If we still desire to visit that past (and why not?), let us do so with a certain sense of freedom from it. We do not have to despise or ridicule it - that is just an adolescent reaction from which one tries to recover, at least by the time one reaches the exalted age of 60! But with a little honest remembering we can all achieve a greater freedom from its allure.

And above all, we can learn to look in it, in that past, for the *alternatives* that it may have contained, all unawares. The alternatives that it could not hear and did not explore, because it was what it was - a majority culture, a civic religion, small-town constantinianism. Even so, in spite of itself, it carried along with it something vastly transcending itself and its mini-moral verities and cramped little orthodoxies. That something, unbidden and often unwelcome, crept into its life and, here and there, functioned as an antiphon to the great, gauche triumph song of village-vintage Christendom. That transcendent Word was heard best, I think, by children and women and men who were hurt most by the words and the deeds that were humanly victorious. This alternative, borne in the bosom of Christendom, because in spite of everything Christendom could not dispense altogether with the Christ: this could be a source of contemplation and recall that might bear much fruit today!

What was it, I wonder, that that one minister of my youth, the one who laughed with my nonconforming father, the one who didn't last long, the exception: what *was* it that he was trying to tell us? What *was* his message?

II

HAS THE CHURCH
A FUTURE?

INTRODUCTION

In the first address, I attempted to characterize Christendom Canadian style, and its breakdown, by employing a variety of narrative theology - or perhaps 'theology as autobiography.' For the present discussion, I shall return to a more discursive and familiar mode of presentation; but I hope that the concreteness of the story - *my* story, through which I tried to remind you of your own stories, your own experience of "where we have been" - will continue to inform your meditation as we attempt to sort out various reactions to the changed status of the churches in our society and to ask, in the light of this, what future we might legitimately hope and work for.

There will be two major segments in my address this morning. In the first, I shall describe what I think are some of the responses to the loss of the future that Christians had been conditioned to assume; and in the second I shall discuss the future I think the church can have, under the heading, "Possibilities and Temptations for a Cruciform Body of Christ."

1. RESPONSES TO THE HUMILIATION OF THE CHURCH

There are, I think, four possible responses to the latter-day disestablishment of Christianity, or what I would prefer to call (with Albert van den Heuvel[1]) "the humiliation of the church" - four primary themes, with variations.

i. Denying It :

The first is of course to deny it. This is a very common response in North America, and the farther south you go on this continent the more common it becomes; so that by the time you hit South Carolina it is not even considered a denial but just a fact: nothing has changed.

Once, shortly after my book, *Has the Church a Future?* [2], came out, someone in the American South who was enthusiastic about it invited me to come and address a Presbytery on the subject. The topic was announced in precisely the same words as it is in the title of the book, and for this event this morning. I had the definite impression that for the vast majority of the clergy and laity assembled there, "Has the church a future?" was a non-question. I even suspect that many had come out (as it is said of the Athenians who came to hear Paul) to see what this babbler would say (Acts 17:18). Could anyone possibly occupy himself with such a question? Even write a book about it? I was never invited to the South again to speak on this particular theme.

Full churches, with congregations belting out gospel hymns and gushing at one another afterwards in packed coffee-hours - such churches are no places to inquire whether the church has a future. I am tempted to think they are no places to inquire *seriously* about much of anything!

[1] *The Humiliation of the Church* (London: S.C.M. Press Ltd., 1967).
[2] Philadelphia: The Westminster Press, 1980.

24

Fortunately for the publishers of this particular book, the question its title asks becomes more existential the farther north you go in North America; so that by the time you reach Newark or Seattle or Toronto you may even be asked to address whole conferences on the subject. This is in fact the *only* book of mine that has sold better in Canada, proportionately, than in the United States. Apparently our cold northern air and our sub rosa cynicism are not conducive to credulity; hence the full churches and swash-buckling Christians are not so numerous amongst us.

Still, even here it is possible to find deniers of the fact of Christendom's effective demise. They will go on at length about some parish they heard of in Mississauga; and indeed there are such parishes, even here. But just for the record we need to recognize that 'here' is not everywhere; and the everywhere-situation runs something like this, so far as Christendom *statistics* are concerned (and I am quoting verbatim from *The World Christian Encyclopaedia*, published by Oxford Press in 1982, after years of painstaking research, and edited by the Rev. Dr. David Barrett)[3]:

> "Between 1900 and 2000, classical Protestantism in the U.S.A. will have shrunk from two-thirds of the population to little more than one-third."

> "The most dramatic changes have been the rise for the first time of atheistic and non-religious masses (now 20.8% of the world population as compared with .2% in 1900) and the precipitous decline of Chinese folk religions and tribal faiths elsewhere."

> "After centuries as the predominant faith of the Northern Hemisphere, especially Europe, christianity as of [1981] had a non-white Majority for the first time in 1200 years."

> "In 1900 two-thirds of Christians lived in Europe and Russia; by 2000, three-fifths of them will live in Africa, Asia and Latin America. *White Westerners cease to be practicing Christians at a rate of 7,600 per day.*"

---

[3]   Nairobi: Oxford University Press, 1982.

"The [so-called] Evangelicals, taken all together, today command a healthy majority of Protestants in the world (157 millions) as well as in the U.S. (59 millions)."

Hans Küng has summarized the situation, quantitatively speaking, in this way: "Of the three billion inhabitants of the earth, only about 950 millions are Christian and only a fraction of those take any practical part in the church."[4]

The specifically Canadian situation was reported on by *MacLean's* in the January 5th, 1987, issue, which presented the results of polls conducted by the magazine on every imaginable theme, especially of course, sex. About religion, the magazine said that its poll had revealed "little evidence for organized religion to cheer about." Those who said religion had become more important in their lives were exactly balanced off by those who said it had become less important (40%, approximately, in both cases). Those who said they were "comfortable" with declining church attendance were balanced off by those who were "uncomfortable" (approximately 50% in both cases). It was in short a nice Canadian balancing act. One datum that seemed to me to say more than all the rest was that 73% of Canadians polled said they were "bothered" by "the growing number of television evangelists," while only 2% were happy about that. I think the Canadian public can congratulate itself on its good taste and foresight. It was turned off the electronic church even before Jimmy Bakker's and Jimmy Swaggart's Elmer Gantry acts began to disturb 'true believing' Americans.

The statistics presented in Reginald Bibby's much-noticed book,[5] while more detailed than those I have just quoted, are substantially the same - which causes one to wonder why Mr. Bibby's book engendered such shocked enthusiasm.

4 "The Freedom of Religions," in Owen C. Thomas, ed., *Attitudes Towards Other Religions*, Lanham: University Press of America, 1986), pp. 195, 199.

5 *Fragmented Gods, Op.cit.*

While we should be aware of such statistics, however, I think they are subtly misleading; for they tempt us to assess the state of Christian faith, which is after all a quality of spirit, by examining quantitative and quantifiable data. Surely the point is not just how many people have left the churches, or how many "still" go to church. The death of Christendom cannot be measured in declining church statistics and givings, even though these may be indicative of some *aspects* of religious attitudes. Neither can the state of the church be assessed by asking people whether they believe in "God", and the divinity of Christ, and life after death, as Bibby does. Even if a hundred percent of Canadians answered yes to all these questions, responsible theology would want to know: *What* God, precisely? and, What do you *mean* by 'divinity'? And do you make any distinction between the pagan teaching about the immortality of the soul and the Christian confession of the 'resurrection of the body'? I have not yet discovered the software that could handle the sort of 'data' that *that* kind of 'research' might produce. Indeed, I have not discovered the 'research' itself!

The state of the Christian Ark is a matter for reflection and *decision*, and there would no doubt be people still denying the humiliation of the church if, like the Titanic, that Ark were to be sinking fast and visibly. But one cannot submit oneself to biblical and serious theological study of the meaning of belief and discipleship and then turn around and assume that the pollsters are the ones best equipped to determine what is what with Christ's flock in the world! The more pertinent investigations of the church, whether they are done under the aegis of the social sciences or of organized religion, must be informed by profound historical and theological knowledge. What American or Canadian people *say* about their belief, or the lack of it, is no more trustworthy today than it was in the Gallilee of Jesus. Relatively large numbers of North Americans, especially U.S. Americans, still *say* they are Christians. But a prominent European theologian says that what she sees parading itself as Christianity in the U.S.A. today, much of it, is what she would prefer to call 'Christofascism.' Touring about in such a world as ours, especially if we are still allowing the Holy Scriptures to be our travel guide, we should never assume that what calls itself Christianity is the genuine article. Most of the right wing political parties in the Western hemisphere have the adjective 'Christian' in their names and slogans. The mere dominance of something called the Christian *religion*, where it may still be found, by no means proves that Christian *faith* has continued intact. Continued . . . ? With Kierkegaard, I'm not even sure it was there before - except as . . . 'the exception.'

ii.   *Attempting to Recover Christendom* :

The second response to the humiliation of the church is to attempt to recover the constantinian model. This too, as I claimed last evening, is an especially North American response. It frequently takes the form of a so-called 'revivalist' approach. Many 'born-again' Christians on this continent are fully agreed that Christendom has been humiliated and decimated. But, they say, this is because Christianity has been ruined by the old, established denominations, or by attitudes and practices that have become dominant within them. Liberalism and humanism have crept into the so-called mainline Protestant and Catholic churches, along with feminism and the ordination of homosexuals and a lot of other unchristian things; so that it is no wonder (they say) that these denominations are in trouble.

But just give us a chance (they say), and we will reverse the trend. And, as we heard in one of the statistics that I quoted from the *World Christian Encyclopaedia* a moment ago, some impressive figures can be adduced in support of this claim. Between 30 and 40 percent of American adults, it is widely proclaimed, now count themselves 'born-againers.' One of them, Pat Robertson, achieved sufficient prestige to believe that he had a chance at the oval office. And all of those who *want* to occupy that particular office - regardless of their belief or the lack of it - must *seem* to be born again, even if only in a mild and decorous and perhaps "Episcopalian" manner.

Recently, when I was meeting with a group of fellow-theologians in the Interchurch Centre in New York City (the so-called God-Box!), one of them pointed out that when that building was opened in 1960, President Eisenhower himself came from Washington to do the honours. And, said my colleague, you can't imagine this happening today. Today, when the White House wants to impress the country with its 'Christianity', it calls upon a quite different segment of the ecclesiastical populace from those denominations involved in the National Council of Churches U.S.A. In fact, as a recent article in *The Christian Century* aptly put it, we ought perhaps to begin now to call the formerly designated 'mainline' churches the 'sideline churches.'

But quite apart from any critique of the *character* of the Christianity represented by those who are most vociferous in their call for the reconstitution of the imperial church, one has to ask what sort of assumptions and strategies would be required to bring this off. For a start, it would be necessary to rule out any serious recognition of religious pluralism. In a church that believes its mission is to try and bring the entire world to Jesus Christ (perhaps, with Campus Crusade or the Southern Baptist Church, "by the year two thousand"), there is no room for acknowledging the truth that may be there in Judaism or Islam or Bahai - except as it serves to buttress the superiority of Christianity.

Again, to reconstitute Christendom along the lines that most of those taking this approach call for it would be necessary to turn back the clock on human scholarship and the consequences of the ideas that it has engendered over the past two centuries at least. Not only Darwin, but also Freud, Marx, Feuerbach, Nietzsche, Hume and countless other 'architects of modern thought' would have to be silenced somehow, along with their present-day followers.

Nearly all modern and contemporary literature - and I do not mean only Erskine Caldwell and James Joyce and Margaret Laurence and J.D. Salinger and Marie-Claire Blais - would have to be put on the index. In fact, the control of *ideas* would be the most important aspect of any such reconstruction of Christendom.

And in case you think this is an exaggeration, I would counsel you to read Jeremy Rifkin's, *The Emerging Order: God in the Age of Scarcity,* [6] followed, maybe, by Margaret Atwood's, *The Handmaid's Tale* .[7] Precisely what has been found necessary (and quite predictably so, if one knows any history) in circles of evangelicalism and fundamentalism where the return to pre-Modern Christianity is attempted, is the construction of whole protective environments deemed 'Christian': Christian schools, Christian Yellow Pages, Christian nightclubs, Christian baby-sitting services, Christian TV and Radio networks, Christian restaurants and hotels, Christian Business Men's organizations, Christian literature racks, even Christian make-up. What such lists indicate implicitly is of course that most of this is just a stained-glass version of common garden-variety Middle Americana. It offers no *real* challenge to the status quo; it is just *Dallas* with less sex - less *overt* sex! Yet it is no trivial affair. For it is not improbable that in order to make the world 'Christian' some of these people are quite willing as a last resort to destroy the non-Christian elements of it, and others (like Hal Lindsey) have already concluded that it can be Christian, anyway, only *after* the Bomb!

iii.   *Behaving 'As If'* :

The third response to the humiliation of the Church is closer to where many of *us* live: it is to carry on as if nothing had happened. The emphasis here is on the words "as if." Most of those who pursue this route know, in their innermost selves, that . . .

---

6   With Ted Howard (New York: G. P. Putnam's Sons, 1979)

7   New York: Fawcett Crest, 1986.

"something happened" (Joseph Heller). They may even speak about it with one another. You can hear them doing so at presbytery and other official meetings of the church - *afterwards*, in little groups of friends. Theological colleges and seminaries often abound with such persons, some of them behind the lectern. They may not believe that the church has much of a future. Or they may be very uncertain about what it is coming to. But they carry on as usual, performing their ministries, preparing for their degrees, teaching their students, maintaining their bureaux. Many of them - should I not say many of us? - watch with concern as inner city congregations become sparser, and more grey-haired. Many take notice when the national budgets of denominations dwindle perceptibly. Many ask why there are so few young people in congregations. But they carry on . . . as if . . . .

I remember that about ten years ago I attended the annual winter conference of the Canadian Theological Students. I had been asked to speak, but instead I interviewed a friend whose experience seemed to me worthy of being heard by the students. This friend, an Anglican priest, had become very weary of carrying on "as if," and he decided to try something different. With the consent of his parish, he trained as an elementary school teacher, and at the end of that year of training he got a job teaching primary school. The arrangement was that he would continue to live in the rectory and do the sorts of priestly things that Anglican clerics have to do; but that the main work of ministry in the congregation would be done by . . . the congregation! He would receive, for his services, a place to live and a small travel allowance.

It transformed the parish. Instead of spending their time wearily and resentfully getting up bazaars and things to pay for the upkeep of their institution, ordinary lay persons now had to conduct classes and visit the sick and the elderly and do most of the things that lay persons have been led to assume only clergy can or ought to do.

31

It seemed to me that the Canadian candidates for ministry should hear about this, so I staged a public conversation with my friend and gradually he related his and his congregation's experience. He did it hesitantly and without pomp, because he was and is a modest man, and, besides, he had no practice in telling about it. For during the eight years that he had been carrying on in this new type of ministry no one had shown the slightest interest in hearing about it. We have talked for several decades now about tent-making ministries, but when it actually happens there is almost a conspiracy of silence!

And now, exposed to it, the students - most of them - reacted in the same way that many of my friend's priestly colleagues had reacted. Indirectly - *very* indirectly, but with the kind of indirectness that is in fact unmistakably direct! - they seemed to say to him: "Don't tell us about this! We want to be part of the profession as it has been. We want manses and pension plans and . . . well yes, why not, the dignity of the office!" What they meant was: Maybe the church in its present form will not last for a long time, but maybe it will last long enough for us. In any case, we are not prepared to risk our own futures for the future of a vision that is still . . . *optional*.

It is of course entirely understandable that people respond in this way, for it requires a great deal of courage to adopt an alternative to the status quo before it becomes absolutely necessary to do so. Nevertheless, it seems to me that the attempt to carry on "as if" is the most questionable response of the three I have thus far described. Because it means that people who *could* do something about the future that the church *could* have are opting out before they even test the alternative *at the imaginative level*. Since they are not *pushed* towards innovation, they fail to develop alternative models of Christian existence beyond the stage of theory, if they even get so far as theory.

iv.   *Seeking Its Positive Meaning* :

There is one other response to the humiliation of the Church. It is the only one, so far as I can see, that can be undertaken with integrity by anyone rooted in the tradition of Jerusalem[8] and wishing to be faithful to the One who took up the cross. I have tried to depict this other way in some of my books and articles - not only in *Has the Church a Future?* but also in my three books on the theology of stewardship and elsewhere.[9] I do not have time to develop here what is, after all, the major *ecclesiological* theme of my work. But I will put it briefly in this way:

The fourth alternative is **(a) to** *accept* **the fact of the church's belittlement, (b) to look for the** *positive meaning* **in this historical event, and (c) to attempt in whatever ways are open to one** *to act upon and live out of the model of the church which emerges from this reflection.* I would like to make short comments on each of these three aspects.

(a) *Accepting the humiliation of Christendom* is hard for all of us, because we have been conditioned by the kinds of assumptions that I tried to exemplify in last evening's presentation of religion and life in my village. As Karl Rahner has put it, we have been taught to believe that the church should baptize, marry, and bury everybody[10]. Moreover, the North American experience has

---

[8]   I have adopted the phrase, "tradition of Jerusalem," from the Canadian philosopher and theologian, the late George P. Grant. Professor Grant used the phrase in juxtaposition with "tradition of Athens" to distinguish the Hebraic and classical Greek components of our civilization. I would like to retain the same connotation; to it, however, I would add that the phrase "tradition of Jerusalem" functions for me as a way of reminding us who are Christians that we are part of a larger and older heritage, and that to comprehend our own message and mission we need to be in dialogue not only with the classical roots of that more expansive tradition (the older Testament) but also the living community, Judaism, for whom that source is also 'Holy Scripture.'

[9]   *The Steward: A Biblical Symbol Come of Age* (New York: Friendship Press, 1982); *The Stewardship of Life in the Kingdom of Death* (Revised Edition); Grand Rapids, Michigan: Wm. B. Eerdmans Publishing House, 1987; *Imaging God: Dominion As Stewardship* (Grand Rapids, Michigan: Wm. B. Eerdmans Publishing House, 1986).

[10] *Mission and Grace: Essays in Pastoral Theology*, Vol. I, trans. by Cecily Hastings (London, Melbourne and New York: Sheed and Ward, 1963), pp. 50 ff.

rendered this ancient constantinian-theodosian assumption even more effective. We are a society that respects winners, and that means Christian winners too: big, successful churches! To put this in the more technical language of theology, we have been indoctrinated in a theological and ecclesiastical triumphalism - a theology of glory (*theologia gloriæ*) that is only made worse by our cultural ideology of success. From the supposed height of being the religious winners, the model of the church as a minority, a diaspora, seems for all the world like losing.

What is required, therefore, if we are even to come to the first stage of this fourth possible response - the state of simply *accepting* the humiliation of the Church - is that we get a new theology - as well, probably, as a new sociology and psychology! In my view, we shall have to exchange the theology of glory for the theology of the cross (*theologia crucis*) as Luther called the true theology.[11] To speak negatively, we shall have to begin to be suspicious - more suspicious than most of us probably are! - about the theology of winning, of success, of great numbers and great deeds. Of Crystal Cathedrals! To speak positively, we shall have to become more convinced than most of us probably are that a theology which finds strength in weakness and significance in littleness and purity in brokenness might have something *entirely significant* to say to our world.

(b) It will help us to make the transition to a cruciform model of the Church, however, if we begin to reflect on the *positive meaning of the church's humiliation*. What is divine Providence trying to teach us in and through this historical eventuality, this reduction of once-proud Christendom over the course of a century or two? Is it not possible that this reduction really *is* providential?

---

[11] For an elaboration of this statement, see my *Thinking the Faith: Christian Theology in a North American Context* (Minneapolis: Augsburg/Fortress, 1989), and *Lighten Our Darkness: Towards an Indigenous Theology of the Cross* (Philadelphia: The Westminster Press, 1976.) I have hinted at some aspects of the *theologia crucis* in the Conclusion of this present work, "Wearing the Colours of the Court."

Surely it would be more justifiable, on *biblical* grounds, to consider the *disestablishment* of the church providential than to consider its *establishment* God's own work (as Pope Sylvester and Bishop Eusebius and others did back there, at the other end of this long process). One does not have to say, with Franz Overbeck, that Christendom was just "a mistake;" but surely we may say, with Emil Brunner, that it involved a rather glaring "misunderstanding." Christians are not, I think, at liberty to assume that God is *wholly* absent from *any* historical occurrence; to do so is to question profoundly the confession of God's sovereignty. But can we on the other hand claim, scripturally, that just because a phenomenon like Christendom lasted for fifteen or sixteen hundred years it was the very will of God, or that it is precisely what Jesus wanted his body on earth to become? I doubt it! I see nothing in the newer Testament, or the older either, to warrant the belief that Jesus Christ intended to found the Holy Roman Empire or the United States of America as a Christian nation! On the contrary, there is a great deal in both testaments to suggest that God is interested chiefly in minorities - remnants, "little flocks here and there" (Rahner), witnessing communities which can help (like salt, and yeast, and little lights in dark places) to "keep human life human" (Paul Lehmann). Surely the biblical story is about the possibilities of littleness. Throughout the continuity of the testaments, as I read them, there is in fact a persistent criticism of bigness, power, and success. "He hath put down the mighty from their seats. . . ." (Luke 1:52). "Let him who stands take heed lest he fall!" (I Cor. 10:12). The Bible takes for granted - what the best human wisdom also knows - that *there are things that majorities, precisely because they are majorities, cannot achieve.* The whole doctrine of election and of the covenant is about this: The possibilities of creative, non-conforming minorities.

So as we contemplate the humiliation of Christendom in the light of the biblical picture of the 'people of God,' we may be enabled to discover a surprisingly positive meaning in it. The same could be said of the tradition as a whole. For there have been witnesses to the cruciform model of the church from the beginning and throughout. Christendom has never been quite without its critics - its ... exceptions! Moreover, if the imperial model of the church is really what the gospel requires, one may ask why it is that after sixteen centuries of pomp and circumstance, holy crusades and pogroms and evangelistic rallies, it has achieved so little by way of real reconciliation within the world. Jesus' temptations were precisely temptations to power and grandeur and success. He rejected this way and took up, instead, the Via Dolorosa. Think about it! - The church for centuries has enthusiastically embraced the very temptations that Jesus rejected. Might it not now, at the end of this experiment in winning, explore with Jesus the way of serving, which has never been very glorious?

(c) The final stage in the transition to the cruciform church is of course to try to *be* such a church. This is the hardest part of all; because even when we can accept the theological propriety of such a transition, and even when we have understood it in some depth, spiritually and humanly speaking, we are still, all of us, products of the constantinian arrangement. Emotionally we are tied to the imperial model of the church even when, intellectually, we recognize its incompatibility with the best traditions of our faith and its inappropriateness to the present historical context.

Moreover, most of us are caught up in the structures of churches formed on Christendom foundations, and in cultural-religious assumptions which are still effective within our society. We are called upon to bless battleships and wars, university convocations and civic undertakings - and to do so strictly within the rubrics of constantinian propriety! (At one of the convocations of my university, I prayed, with [I thought] great propriety, for peace; afterwards people wanted to know who "the radical" was). Christians are still expected to undergird, cultically, the pursuits and values of the dominant culture, and not to buck the system. We are, moreover, most of us, economically and professionally dependent upon these same structures and assumptions; and our courage is regularly and effectively bridled by our physical needs and family commitments and parish connections and a host of other things.

Besides, as I said in my first address, we are still vastly tempted by the old, established model of Christendom. We dream about it still. The good things that were part of it constantly blunt our recognition of its great unfaithfulness to Jesus Christ, and we end in an all-too-Canadian balancing act which precludes decisive thought and action.

Perhaps most of us will continue throughout our ministries to be torn between the two images of the body of Christ, recognizing the scriptural and theological soundness of the one, but feeling impotent to slough off the other, and so embodying in ourselves a certain duplicity and knowing ourselves to be open to the charge of hypocrisy.

I know situations in both the Second and Third worlds where Christians have not been given the choice of holding onto the old model, but have been thrust into the new willy nilly; and I somehow envy them. As my friend Milan Opocenski of Prague says, "Our situation is the normal one for the Church. Yours is abnormal." First world Christians, and especially those of us who still find ourselves in the "sideline" denominations of what is nonetheless the dominant culture are in some ways, of all contemporary followers of the Christ, most to be pitied. In East Germany and in Black South Africa, Christian ministers and theologians have been forced out of their constantinian security. We, if we are to do it, must *choose* to do it. And how do you choose . . . the way of the cross? How do you become willingly, and without being pushed by anything but the divine Spirit, 'the people of the Cross' - *Ecclesia crucis* ?

There is no easy answer to this question, and I am not going to attempt one. I will only say, as my final point for today, what the possibilities and temptations of that way seem to me to be.

2. POSSIBILITIES & TEMPTATIONS FOR A CRUCIFORM BODY OF CHRIST

i. *Authenticity.*

First the possibilities. To begin with, the choice of a cruciform model of the church offers us the possibility of a kind of authenticity that is seldom experienced in imperial or cultural forms of Christianity. I could illustrate this in many ways, but let this suffice for now - it is a quotation from that 19th century maverick who first noticed the incongruity between Christ and Christendom, the "ugly duckling," Soren Kierkegaard:

> In the magnificent cathedral the Honourable and Right Reverend Geheime-General-Ober-Hof Prädikant, the elect favourite of the fashionable world, appears before an elect company and preaches with emotion upon the text he himself elected: "God hath elected the base things of the world, and the things that are despised" - *and nobody laughs.*[12]

Who has not felt a twinge of phoniness as he or she stood in some well-appointed, well-heeled, perhaps pseudo-gothic structure of the church and read to an audience (yes, audience) of well-dressed, affluent North American church-goers some biblical words about the suffering of the people of God, how not many were rich or learned or famous, how many were slaves, nobodies, wandering Arameans, broken-spirited sinners whose very goodness was "as filthy rags," human beings saved by sheer grace because nothing

---

[12] *Attack Upon Christendom* , trans. by Walter Lowrie (Boston: The Beacon Press, 1944; p. 181)

else *could* save them. . . etc.? From the standpoint of persons who have known, throughout the years of their serious Christian awareness, something about the discrepancy between the biblical picture of the church and the church as it has actually been and (yes) wanted to be, it is a wonderful relief whenever we find ourselves in situations where we can recognize some genuine hint of correspondence between our biblically based ecclesiology and the empirical church. This is why so many of our contemporaries have found a new lease on the Christian life when they became acquainted with churches in clearly *disestablished* situations - in El Salvador, or Nicaragua, or South Africa, or China, or in poor urban ghettos of our own large cities.

ii. *Orientation to Truth:*

Secondly, the adoption of the cruciform shape of the church holds out the prospect that the church may become a really *prophetic* voice in society. As I have said earlier, there are things that religious majorities cannot do. And one of them is that they can rarely if ever tell the truth *about themselves.* They cannot tell what their power and their need to sustain and enhance their power does to others. They cannot tell the truth about the victims of their own pursuits. They are bound to keep up the ideology of the dominant social stratum, of which they are merely the cultic dimension. Individuals within such majority ecclesiastical structures may rise above the ideologies; but they can only do so by rising above - and therefore alienating themselves from - the ecclesial structures too. Like the glorious exception of ministry in my childhood, most of them will not "last long."

As a majority religion, the official cult of the official culture, Christianity has always been forced (not only by external forces, but by its own preferred relationship with power) to legitimate and reinforce power. Those who live in kings' houses seldom become critics of the king's court or champions of its victims. Even in ancient Israel, which, in a sense unique in history, *made room* for the prophet, the prophetic office was always dangerous and never popular. Seldom were prophets permitted to chastise their host institutions, the kingship and the official priesthood. To move into the diaspora situation, to leave the king's house (the White House!) is no easy transition, after 16 centuries!

But there is at least this advantage in it: that it may be possible then to become truthful.

There is a wonderful German word - *Wahrheitsorientierung* - 'orientation towards the truth.' Christendom at its best was not, I think, orientated towards the Lie; sometimes, indeed, it demonstrated unusual integrity, as when Hildebrand made the Emperor Henry IV do penance for his crimes at Canossa. But, for the most part, Christendom has not been orientated towards *the truth*, either. It has been orientated towards diplomacy--and as Paul Scherer used to tell us in homiletics classes, "Three generations of tact *make* a liar." Listening to many sermons over the last half century, I have often wondered what would happen if somebody called a spade a spade. Sometimes I wondered this when I was myself the preacher.

iii. *Mission as Service:*

Finally, the prospect of the church as diaspora, as 'people of the cross,' means the possibility that the life of the Christian community will become (what we have frequently announced that it is!) the life of a servant people. Rhetorically, the Christian establishment has always known the power of the language of service. The most powerful popes in Christendom have been happy to apply to themselves the title, *Servus servorum Dei* [servant of the servants of God]. We Protestants have our own ways of employing this same rhetoric to good effect. So one must not count too much on the language alone. What better way is there to ingratiate oneself with power than to claim to desire nothing but servanthood!

In fact the service of the church has all too consistently been self-service. Think of the way we have understood our mission. It is virtually impossible to study the history of Christian missions without concluding that what it is really all about is Christian expansionism. The great ages of Mission, like the 19th century, are identified in most histories of the church as the epochs during which the Christian religion took over more of the territory and population of the world - often, as in the history of our own continent, in the wake of 'Christian' armies and businessmen!

Today we are living in a world that is mortally threatened by predators who announce their intention to serve the world. They spread their influence by whatever means they can, chiefly through violence of a covert or overt nature. God's good earth does not need any more such predators - and especially not predators that in God's own name, and the name of the crucified one, seek to expand their sphere of power. A world that is suffering multifold crises needs only service - true service: the kind of service that the Samaritan offered the one who fell amongst thieves. Service that does not have strings attached. Service which can think clearly about peace and justice and the integrity of creation - without wanting to have its own reward for such altruism, or its 'commercial' at the end. In the kingdom of death that our world has become, the mission of the church must be understood as the stewarding of life: not the life of the church, but the life of the world, of creation. And this is possible only for a cruciform church - a church which does not count its own humiliation too great a price to pay for the *shalom* of God's beloved world.

iv. *Self-Righteousness:*

There are also *temptations* for the cruciform church. How could there not be temptations for such a church, when the One on whose life it is patterned - whose life it represents in the world - was himself tempted, profoundly, even on the verge of Golgotha, even on the cross itself!

I shall end this statement with what will have to be a mere nod in the direction of these temptations - not because I enjoy doing so, but because there *are* temptations and dangers for such a church; because these temptations and dangers are experienced by all the people I know who live in such churches; and because *it is precisely on account of these temptations and dangers that we know we are not, after all, simply courting a romantic ideal but pursuing a real alternative.* A church without temptations, without dangers, would be no church, just for the same reasons that a theology without risks would be no theology but only ideology.

There is first the temptation to self-righteousness. All those throughout the history of the Christian movement who have come near to the sort of *authenticity* about which I spoke a moment ago; all those from Stephen to Dietrich Bonhoeffer who have had to follow dramatically and all the way 'the way of the cross' - they have all known this temptation. It is a heady thing to think oneself ... *truly Christian!* Paul understood how attractive this ideal was. .. and therefore he spoke about 'the thorn' (II Cor. 12:7), undoubtedly - whatever its *physical* aspect - a spiritual antidote to his own spiritual pride.

I have never known anyone well who came near what I am calling the cruciform form of the church who did not suffer from the temptation to self-congratulation - and sometimes frankly yielded to it. You can find it in most of the accounts of the martyrs. You can find it in the writings of Martin Luther, and of Martin Luther King.

How easy it would be, and is, for churches that have left behind, or been forced out of, the constantinian mold to compare themselves very favourably indeed with all those centuries of ecclesiastical play-acting and "misunderstanding!" (Brunner). But possibly no temptation is more deadly to the faith of the Christ than the temptation to exceptional holiness: to do, as T.S. Eliot brilliantly put it into the mouth of one of those martyrs, Thomas a Becket, - "to do the right thing for the wrong reason," this is "the greatest treason."[13]

v. *Mediocrity:*

Another temptation of the disestablished church is the temptation to mediocrity. I think we are already witnessing something of this temptation as we stand, in our "sideline" churches, on the brink of cultural disinheritance. We are liable to give way all too easily to little ambitions. Misinterpreting the possibilities of littleness and powerlessness, we interpret our failures, our capitulations to laziness, our lack of struggle with ourselves and the world as if they were virtues. In ethics we give way to trendiness; in theology we cease to struggle with the best and most difficult and most challenging worldly alternatives to the Christian gospel. In art and liturgy and song we substitute sentimentality and *Kitsch* and folksiness for the quest for beauty and profundity.

It should not be forgotten that for all its theological ambiguity and compromise, Christendom begat great art (Bach, Rembrandt), and great thought (St. Thomas, Ockham), and great moral discourse (Augustine, Calvin). The wise and disciplined thinkers and apologists of our past sought out and did honest intellectual battle with the *best* representatives of worldly wisdom. The preachers of the Protestant tradition were in the best sense often truly *learned* persons. The architects of the magnificent cathedrals of the West were skilled and dedicated artists and engineers. Surely the transition to a cruciform church ought not to mean - need not mean - that *that* must go, along with the pomp and pretense that regularly accompanied all that. Surely the orientation to truth must always also mean an orientation to *beauty*, and not the substitution of banality for excellence.

vi. *Ghettoization:*

Finally there is a temptation that we already know intimately,

---

[13] *Murder In The Cathedral*, Part I, in *The Complete Poems and Plays* (New York: Harcourt, Brace and Company, 1930 etc.); p. 196.

most of us, even on the edge of diaspora existence: the temptation to become a ghetto, to hide our light under a bushel, to seek refuge in cosy circles of "fellowship." Turned out of the king's house, the church of the centuries may come to enjoy too well its own little hovels. Refused dialogue with the powerful and the learned, it may come to like too well its little chats with like-minded resenters of the dominant culture, having their little revenges on the edge of history. Sensing that it cannot claim its customary place amongst the movers and shakers, the humiliated church may settle down comfortably enough with other outcasts. One does not have to speculate about this. It has already happened in many places.

Against this temptation, the church of the future will have to remember the prophets - from Samuel to John the Baptist to Reinhold Niebuhr. Their removal from power did not mean that they ceased to prophesy in the face of power or to strive for the public good.

Above all, the church of the future will have to remember Jesus, who taught in the open, and challenged the chiefest of priests and rulers, and was crucified in a public place. For it was *the world* that God "so loved" in him, through him. And his body, the Church, will only be conformed to him, its head - that is, it will only acquire a *cruciform form* - if it always resists the temptation to build tabernacles in dark and sacred places and returns, again and again, to the marketplace, to burning Rome, to the uncertain streets of the *civitas terrena.*

III

THEOLOGICAL DIRECTIVES FOR A DIASPORA CHURCH

INTRODUCTION: BEYOND CHRISTENDOM

I must begin this final lecture in the series, "The Future of the Church: Where are We Headed?", by asking your indulgence: I have made a slight, though I think perhaps clarifying change in the title. To announce as the burden of a single address - as it is announced in your brochure - that one is going to deliver "A Theology for the Diaspora Church" is not only presumptuous, it is also contextually imprecise.

For it suggests that our ecclesiastical existence in the so-called main-stream Christian denominations of the First World today is already that of a diaspora - little flocks here and there; creative minorities; salt, yeast, light in dark places. I do not believe that is our present reality. I do think, however, that something like that is what we might *become*, or help give birth to; and it is towards that 'becoming' that I want to address these thoughts. Hence my new title is, "Theological Directives for a Diaspora Church."

In an earlier lecture, I said that the state of the church is a matter for reflection and decision. It is not something that can be determined by pollsters! Each of us has to ask him- or herself, and one another, where we have been, where we are, and where we are going. This is part of what it means to be a serious Christian, to be 'on the Way.' As with any other journey, part of what is involved in this pilgrimage of faith is trying to apprehend where we are in relation to where we have come from and where we hope to go.

As I myself have tried to assess our present reality as First World churches stemming especially from classical Protestant sources, I have had to conclude that we are currently in a state of radical transition. That observation is of course a commonplace, since transition is 'the name of the game,' until we realize - as I endeavoured to illustrate in the two previous lectures - that the current religious transition, which has been under way for well over a century, is a momentous one, and has, in fact, all the proportions of a crisis. So momentous is this ecclesiastical 'paradigm shift,' if you will, that it is comparable in scope and implication only to the historical transition that occurred at the other end - the beginning - of the process that is now ending: that is, the Constantinian-Theodosian Establishment of the Christian religion in the 4th century of the common era. To that *Establishment*, which has been implemented in the West in both *de jure* and *de facto* variations on the theme for more than fifteen centuries, there now corresponds an equally decisive, though less pinpointable *Disestablishment*. To that beginning there now comes into view an ending - what the East German theologian Günther Jakkob three decades ago called "the End of the Constantinian Era." That ending is of course more visible - inescapably visible - in some places, like Günter Jakkob's German Democratic Republic, than in others. But nowhere, not even in the various North American 'Bible Belts,' can it be wholly ignored.

Such a transition means many things. One aspect of it is of course quantitative: we are moving from a majority to a minority status - fewer people, less money and property, less power and influence. That aspect of the change can be detailed by certain types of investigation, which answer certain types of questions - or at least make the questions clearer. But the quantitative depletion of Christendom is neither the only, nor is it in itself and such the most significant aspect of this watershed. Far more perplexing are the many intangibles cast up by this changed and changing status of Christianity in the Western world.

Above all, the internal and external events which comprise this great transition put us into a state of grave uncertainty about our identity and our purpose as a religion. Our future! *"Where are we going?"* How can we think of ourselves, our mission, our message, under such historical circumstances? We are conspicuously confused about these things. So much of what we *have* thought about ourselves in the past is dependent upon quantitative factors for its confirmation. For all intents and purposes, we have measured Christian faithfulness by the same criteria of success as are applied by the other institutions of our host culture, by government, by business, by the professions. Churches naturally seem to us to be spiritually vital only if they are economically viable; if they are marked by steady growth in members, property, and community influence we hold them up as examples for all to emulate. Christian mission and evangelism is regularly regarded as 'a movement of the Spirit' if it creates a stir in the media and brings in many new converts. Preachers must really be preaching the Word if they attract large congregations, and seminaries must be excellent if they enroll more students than other seminaries. And so on!

But suddenly these quantitative proofs of ecclesiastical well-being have faltered (actually, we ought to have known about their faltering long before Mr. Bibby presented his latest statistics!); and what this signifies for us is infinitely more shocking than the numbers as such. The numbers are in fact significant only because of their implicit but unquantifiable messages! In North America, which never enjoyed the dubious benefits of the old legal establishments of Europe with their guarantees of ecclesiastical power written into church-state relations, quantities, numbers, *large* numbers, have always functioned for us to ensure our *de facto* cultural establishment. So long as we could produce impressive statistics of church membership and attendance, of financial giving, of wheeling and dealing in high places, we could seem secure as the chosen cult of the chosen culture. So the message hidden in the numbers is the message of our disestablishment. But disestablishment does not only mean the loss of numbers. It means the loss of a whole way of being the church, of a whole theology!

For every aspect of Christian theology - not only our ecclesiology, but also our doctrines of God, of the Christ, of salvation, of the Kingdom and eschatology - *every* aspect of our theology was profoundly affected by the fact of Christian Establishment. An imperial religion had to have an imperial theology, and empires do not go in for crucified criminals as their major cultic symbol! They prefer eagles - or at least *vindicated and conquering* formerly-crucified criminals! Christian Establishment, wherever it has pertained, has been required to adjust its theology, its christology, its ecclesiology, its eschatology and all to the rhetorical or real values of its host societies.

What therefore is challenged by the gradual but decisive *disestablishment* of the Christian religion is precisely our theology. To make good the prospect of becoming a prophetic minority, a diaspora, we are obliged to acquire what amounts to a whole new theology - new, or perhaps very old! Older than Christendom.

This constitutes an almost overwhelming challenge for the churches - and who cannot sympathize with ordinary Christians throughout the world today, especially in the First World, who are terribly confused about 'where we are going.' For however inadequately they have been catechized in the subtleties of the faith, the Christian laity have been given this one lesson over and over again for centuries: namely, that while the church may require of them a *"higher"* morality, it is precisely of the same fundamental order as the duties and verities taught them by their culture at large. Like the almost identical roles of church and school in my village. We should not be surprised, therefore, when members of The United Church of Canada, hearing that their church wants them to embrace truths and moral directives and social visions *significantly different* from those of their host culture, are assailed by feelings of radical disorientation.

While it is unfortunate and even in a way tragic that little of this has been effectively communicated to the laity as a whole, it is nonetheless true that many Christians in many parts of the world, both lay persons, clergy and professional theologians, have taken up this challenge to rethink Christian theology in a basic way - and that they have done so ever since the humiliation of Christendom first manifested itself at the beginning of the 19th century. One could even say that all or most of the creative theology that has been done for the past two centuries has been done in response to this very challenge, this sense of the demise of Christendom. Schleiermacher, Kierkegaard, Barth, Tillich, Bonhoeffer, Reinhold and Richard Niebuhr, Karl Rahner, Gustavo Gutierrez, Jose Miguez-Bonino, James Cone, Gregory Baum, Dorothee Sölle, Rosemary Ruether and countless others have worked out their theological testimonies in the way that they have because they were conscious of the fact that Christianity no longer exists in the Western world as a foregone conclusion, the official cult of the official culture. Their creativity as theologians has been determined by this fundamental realization, expressed in relation to the specific problems and possibilities of their different contexts.

But while minorities within the churches have tried to face the humiliation of Christendom honestly and rethink the faith accordingly, the response of most Christians - and particularly North American Christians - has followed another course (predictably enough, I think, in the light of our failure to be a truly democratic and truly teaching church). The typical response of most Christians to the changed circumstances of the church in the modern world has manifested, I think, two distinct facets - but they are two sides of the same coin: One side entails the repression or suppression of any existentially gripping awareness of the transition in question; and the other is that, when it becomes impossible to close one's eyes to the end of the constantinian era any longer, one determines to try all the harder to achieve the goals that 15 centuries of imperial Christianity taught one to consider basic. It seems to me that the considerable and (in my view) unwarranted stir created by Reginald Bibby's *Fragmented Gods* in several Canadian Protestant churches was directly related to these two common reactions to the transitional situation. On the one hand, Mr. Bibby put before the churches data about the diminished state of Christendom that they could not ignore (this was the requisite shock factor of the book); and then he told us how, if only we would package our gospel-product more attractively, with a better eye to public demand, we could find an enormous market for it and thus *re*-establish the very Christendom whose disestablishment (at the quantitative level) he and his 'researchers' had busily tabulated for us. If nothing else, the book betokens a clever reading of the anxieties and religious predispositions of Canadian Protestants!

My own intention - both in these lectures and in most of my written work - is quite different. I too would like to contribute something to the Christian awareness of this momentous historical transition, and at every level of it, not only the quantitative - least of all the quantitative! But I have no desire whatsoever to do this as a way of shocking us into attempts to reconstitute Christendom. My hope, rather (and I think it is in line with the projects of most of those whom I named a moment ago, and many others whom I did not name, including many whose names will never appear in books of the history of Christian thought!) is to help us to make the transition into the diaspora situation, and to do so creatively and courageously.

We *can* do this creatively and courageously - not because we are by nature capable of such high intellectual and spiritual feats (who can actually *will* humility!) but because "the Spirit helps us in our weakness" (Rom. 8:26).

I do not hesitate in this connection to introduce the Holy Spirit, for I do not for a moment regard the humiliation of Christendom as a mere historical accident. I am too much of a Calvinist for that! Something quite *providential* is going on in this reduction of once-proud Christendom. I believe that *God* is at work in this act of disestablishment. It would not be the first time that the God of the Scriptures engaged in such a tactic; indeed, if one follows the history of ancient Israel carefully, one might even conclude that disestablishment is a regular habit of Yahweh! And I believe, further, on the grounds of this same sacred history, that it is possible for 'the people of this God,' through grace, to involve *themselves* in this transitional process in a way that is both faithful and fruitful.

There is, in short, *a very special invitation to discipleship in these events and changes*, even in the statistics! It is an invitation to take up the cross, that is, to submit to the "decrease" that is *Christ's* way (not Caesar's) of "increase" (John 3:30). We shun the invitation to become a diaspora church, we refuse to be humiliated (van den Heuvel), because, from the perspective of the deeply entrenched sociological, religious and theological assumptions of 15 centuries of 'Christendom,' the various humiliations and deliberate reductions that are involved in this process can only seem like failure. But there are criteria of obedience and authenticity to which Christians are bound other than the mostly quantitative tests of 'success' that we derive from the chequered career of imperial Christianity in the Western world! Having, for by far the greater share of our history, enthusiastically taken up (and to what avail?) the very temptations that Jesus Christ overcame - temptations to power, to the spectacular, to supranatural triumph! - why should we not at last attempt to take seriously that his way really is what he said it was, what he himself exemplified: namely, the way of the cross, of servanthood and prophetic vigilance on the part of "little flocks," of a weakness that is powerful only in sacrificial love?

In what remains of this address I want to outline in the briefest possible way some of the barriers that I think we shall have to 'get beyond' if we are going to accept this invitation and make this transition to the diaspora in a creative way. In the two previous lectures, and in this one to the present, I have been claiming in effect that the most important obstacle for us to overcome is Christendom itself, as it impinges still upon our fantasies. We should cease allowing ourselves to be taunted by that past, cease building our visions for the future on its crumbling foundations, cease judging our present reality by the standards it has set. Christendom was *always* ambiguous, and it was never so golden as we imagine! More important, to achieve it the Christian movement had to compromise its new-covenantal charter in truly abysmal and far-reaching ways. Perhaps for a time it 'gained the whole world,' or at least the West; but did it not also in the process perhaps (as is usual with these kinds of triumphs) 'lose its soul?'

Let us therefore as the first directive for our future appropriation of this new invitation to Christian discipleship *get beyond Christendom.*

1. BEYOND TOLERANCE

Secondly, we are called in the context of this pluralistic culture to get beyond tolerance.

In 1989 many of us, I hope, will observe the 300th anniversary of one of the great achievements of anglosaxon Christendom, the Act of Toleration of 1689. This was a remarkable event in

British history, which distinguished the course of religion in anglosaxon cultures from that of societies which evolved out of the religious upheavals of continental Europe. While not everyone in Christendom was tolerated (Roman Catholics and Unitarians were excluded), people were free to dissent from the majority. To be ... exceptions.

And surely that must be regarded as a very Good Thing! But today we are required - and by law! - to extend the spirit of tolerance not only to the *Christians* whom this historic Act excluded, but to greater and greater numbers of persons "who are not [not at all!] of this fold." More than that, we are required by 'the law of Christ,' which is love, to recognize that tolerance is not enough.

The toleration of persons of other faiths and opinions is of course superior to arrogance; but it is hardly synonymous with love. 'Tolerance,' Reinhold Niebuhr used to tell us, 'is the tacit decision to look past one another.' We will allow you to have your beliefs, strange as they are, *false* as they are, because we really do not care, finally, what you think; and we would ask you to reciprocate. In this way we can achieve civility, if not exactly social harmony.

This, in varying degrees and modes, some liberal, some conservative, is approximately what we have managed, most of us, so far. Live and let live. It *may* be good enough, legally and politically, for the pluralistic society; but it is not good enough theologically. It is not good enough for the one who did *not* say "Tolerate your neighbour," but "Love your neighbour."

Getting beyond tolerance of other religious faiths is not only important for those other faiths, it is important for Christians themselves. If the diaspora church is to overcome the typical temptation of minorities - the temptation to self-righteous ghettoization - it will have to find a way of being vis-à-vis these 'others' quite different from the way of tolerance. It will have to approximate real love for them. And it is clear enough what barrier stands in the way to the achievement of the spirit of love which belongs to the church in the diaspora situation. It is the sense, ingrained in us by centuries of a virtual monopoly on the souls of human beings, that ours is the *true* faith. It is the exclusivity that is born of theological triumphalism, which in turn is the natural child of religious imperialism.

And it is the quite natural bi-product of this *theologia gloriœ*, fear: fear, namely, that if once we admit the possibility of truth in the faith of the others, we shall *ipso facto* jeopardize and relativize our own!

Dear colleagues: the invitation to discipleship that is extended to us in this historical moment is precisely an invitation, and indeed a command, to rid ourselves once for all of these "pretentions of finality" (Reinhold Niebuhr). It is an invitation and command to exchange our inheritance of theological triumph for the modesty that Karl Barth rightly said inheres in this most modest science, Christian theology, and must do so because of its object, who is no object but is Subject[1]. It is an invitation and command to overcome our entrenched 'theologies of glory' by the 'theology of the cross.' The Disestablishment of Christendom, creatively entered into by faithful Christians, must entail the detriumphalization of the Christian faith and theology.

Certainly we have to do with Truth! But we do not *possess* it! To 'have to do' with this Truth is precisely *not* to possess it! Earlier, I reminded you of a marvellous German word, *Wahrheitsorientierung*: orientation towards the Truth. Faith in Jesus Christ is *orientation* towards Truth, not *having* it but *being turned* towards it - more often than not, against one's own will! Against the comfortable half-truth and the downright falsehood that one prefers, against the Lie that is constantly courted and propagandized by the kingdoms of this world and the glory of them! Jesus did not say

---

[1] *Evangelical Theology: An Introduction*, trans. by Grover Foley (New York, Chicago, San Francisco: Holt, Rinehart and Winston, 1963), p. 7.

to his original disciples, "Here is the Truth. Write it down!" He said rather, "I *am* the Truth" - because God's truth is a living Truth, and therefore not containable in 'truths'; God's Word is a living Word and therefore not capturable in words. At the centre of our faith there is: Jesus Christ. Not our christologies; not Chalcedon; not the soteriology of Calvin or Wesley; not liberation theology, either. And if we do not know that Jesus Christ himself *relativizes* our christologies and our theologies, then we Protestants have not yet understood what Tillich rightly identified as 'the Protestant principle.'[2]

Only that church which knows profoundly that its very confession of Jesus as 'Sovereign and Saviour' precludes any claim to the sovereignty of its own *belief system* will be in a position to open itself to the beliefs of others - and hence to the others themselves. Only that church which is orientated towards a Truth that it knows it can never possess, which *stands under* a Word that it will never fully *understand*: only such a church will get beyond tolerance and move towards love.

2. BEYOND RELIGIOUS SIMPLISM

A third obstacle to the acceptance of the invitation to becoming a creative dispersion of prophetic faith in First World societies in general, and in North America in particular, is a phenomenon that I call religious simplism. For millions of persons on this Continent, both Christians and non-Christians, the Christian religion has been identified with its most simplistic articulations. By simplistic I do not mean simple. Simple is a word with a deep and honourable connotation. God, said the medieval theologians, is 'simple,' - meaning that God is *one*, and therefore not divided, not capricious,

---

[2] See the various references to this 'Principle' in Tillich's *Systematic Theology* (Chicago: University of Chicago Press, Vol. I, 1951; Vol. II, 1957; Vol. III, 1963), and in *The Protestant Era* (Chicago: University of Chicago Press, 1948).

not hampered by the duplicitous thought and warring emotions that beset human beings. True simplicity, wherever it is found, is truly profound.

By simplistic I mean the reduction of something profound to a straightforward but conceptually crude version of itself. This is usually done (and I do not suggest that it is done *intentionally*) by eliminating from the more penetrating understanding of a concept any element of the paradoxical. To use other language, it is achieved by substituting for dialogical or dialectical thought about a given reality a straight linear approach. For example: an ancient proverb wisely states that "the line between love and hate is as thin as a razor's edge." That is dialectical thinking. Hollywood, in thousands of Grade B movies, presented sentimental portrayals of love in which there was no hint of love's antithesis: that is linear thought. It is simplistic because it oversimplifies and falsifies reality, which is always full of unpredictable combinations and strange admixtures of opposites.

The simplism of popular forms of Christianity on this Continent can be illustrated by reference to *four central aspects of Reformation Protestantism.*

(i) The Reformers taught that we are justified by grace, through faith. For them, faith meant trust - *fiducia* [3] - and they were wise enough about human nature to know that trust, whether it is in God or in other persons, is always dogged by distrust, and therefore that faith and doubt are not strangers to one another, but partners. "Lord I believe, help my unbelief" (Mark 9:24). Religious simplism not only distinguishes sharply between belief and unbelief, faith and doubt, but it usually defines faith as assent to certain religious propositions: faith as *assensus* rather than *fiducia.* Those who accept the proferred dogmas of the group as true are believers, those who do not are unbelievers. Thus the *sola fide* of the

---

3   See the further discussion of 'trust' in the section IV.

Reformation is transmuted into the insidious notion of the 'true believer.' Faith has become credulity.

(ii) The Reformers also insisted upon the authority of the Bible, and indeed the *sola scriptura* principle is rightly called the 'formal principle' of the Reformation, and is as such second only to the 'material principle,' which is the aforementioned doctrine of justification by grace through faith. But for neither Luther, Calvin, nor Zwingli did biblical authority connote what it does for biblical literalism in North America today. The identification of the Bible *as* the Word of God is a simplistic version of the profound Reformation teaching that the scriptures witness in a unique way to the *living* Word, which no mere words can contain.

(iii) In the realm of *Christian ethics*, the classical sources of Protestantism make much of the concept of 'obedience.' The obedience required of the disciple community is obedience to its living Lord, whom the divine Spirit makes present to faith. As in the prophetic tradition of ancient Israel, it is "the Voice" - *God's* command - for which the community of faith is to listen. Moral precepts - laws - may certainly help belief to distinguish between God's voice and the voices of false shepherds. But the laws must not be so rigidly absolutized as effectively to replace the Voice, the active Spirit of God. This is why Jesus could feel free to interpret the law in new and, for many, offensive ways. Religious simplism removes from the concept of obedience the element of tension between letter and Spirit. Obedience becomes a matter of conforming to a quite explicit moral code, endorsed, it may be, by a 'moral majority.'

(iv) In its understanding of *the church and its relation to the state*, the Protestant Reformation manifested, it is true, a number of differing patterns. Yet in all the forms of the Reformation there is strong evidence of that same 'Protestant principle' to which I alluded a moment ago - namely, the refusal to attribute ultimacy to anything less than the Ultimate, i.e. to God. So even in denominations of Protestantism fundamentally loyal to states, there has been a certain vigilance; because, as John Knox for instance insisted, rulers may be or become tyrants, and as such must be resisted. Religious simplism on our continent easily aligns itself with the power of the dominant culture and of government. This, as Margaret Atwood has demonstrated so imaginatively in her disutopic novel, *The Handmaid's Tale* [4], may be the most dangerous aspect of religious simplism in North America. A nuclear and economic superpower, persuaded by its most vociferous religious backers of its superior righteousness over against an 'ungodly' enemy can pose an incalculable threat to life on this planet.

Now, religious simplism has been aided and abetted in North America today by numerous factors - including the chief medium of communication, television, which favours simplism at every level; but this oversimplification and sloganization of the faith is by no means an exclusively contemporary phenomenon. Surely the truth is that the process of theological reductionism is inherent in the constantinian model of the church. Wherever it is assumed that Christianity should be the religion of the majority, hopefully of the totality, the Christian religion must needs be reduced to simplistic versions of itself. This is not only because it can never be realistically supposed that everyone will be serious enough about the faith to bother exploring its profundities; it is also - and I think more so - because wherever those profundities *are* explored seriously, they are bound to raise questions that are, to say the least, awkward for any majority culture to handle!

To illustrate: a theological tradition which continuously raises critical questions about authority, and in the name of the *victims* of authority, will hardly function smoothly as a majority religion. It will have to be simplified. The vigilance of the prophets against the misuse of power, the Bible's "preferential option for the poor," the critique of property and privilege that is inescapably

4 Op.cit.

there in this tradition - such emphases will have to be minimized, perhaps through reduction to mere rhetoric, and the teachings with which, in the scriptures, they are held in dialectical tension (such as the injunction to *respect* the governing authorities and the *universal* outreach of divine love, to rich as well as poor) - these will have to be maximized. In short, when the Christian movement allowed itself to become an imperial religion it gave way to the preference of majorities for straightforward and uncomplicated cultic endorsement of their own regnant values and pursuits.

Conversely, the *dis*establishment of the Christian religion - if it is to be achieved creatively and not allowed simply to 'happen'! - requires of those who remain within the church that they become theologically *serious*! It requires this not only of theologians and clergy, but of all Christians. We shall have to recover the deepest wisdom of the tradition of Jerusalem - and it *is* wisdom. It is a travesty of this wisdom when it is reduced to biblicistic and pietistic slogans that have all the depth of singing commercials! It is like casting fake pearls before guileless swine! Not that the people on the receiving end of electronic evangelism *are* swine, in any sense, but they are being treated as if they were mindless - wholly incapable of serious thought - and could only imbibe the leftovers of an already truncated version of Christian faith.

It is by no means an easy thing to get beyond religious simplism; because, if my analysis has any validity, religious simplism is the ideational backbone of the culture-religion called Christianity. To get beyond this simplism, we must first desire to get beyond Christendom itself. But if we do not will to become theologically serious; if as a whole people and movement we do not struggle to find 'the reason for the hope that is in us,' Christendom will eventually disappear anyway, being found inadequate to speak to the deepest quest of the human spirit, the quest for meaning.

3.   BEYOND THE 'ISSUES'

Finally (for the present) I feel constrained to say something that I would in many ways prefer not to say, because it is susceptible to gross misunderstanding. But I think that it must be said, and particularly within ecclesial communities like our own, which in so many ways seem to me to be open to the invitation to leave the securities of Christendom for the unknown risks of the wilderness, the *terra incognita* that is called "future."   It is not so difficult for us to think about overcoming religious simplism, because (perhaps with a faulty self-knowledge) we consider that to be, mainly, the problem of other manifestations of the Christian religion on this continent.   But one of the abiding marks of the church is *self-criticism*:   the judgment begins at the household of faith, and especially at 'critical' junctures in its life God permits that household to participate in God's own *krisis* [judgement] (I Peter 4:17).

What I want to say is something like this: I think that we must get beyond the identification of Christian faith with . . . 'issues.' This is so subtle an aspect of our topic that I hesitate even to mention it. It would be *entirely* against my intention in doing so if anyone were to hear me saying that the churches are paying too much attention to issues like peace, justice, ecology, unemployment, human rights, gender discrimination, homophobia, and so on. The truth of the matter is precisely the opposite: namely, that while significant *minorities* in the churches have identified such ethical and social issues as being the business of Christian faith and witness, the majority of people in our Canadian middle-class churches seem either blithely unaware of the threats to life present in these great instabilities of the age, or content to let others tend to them, or (in the case of *some* of these issues) shocked and incensed that the church should even raise them.

All the same, the problem does not lie entirely 'out there' - in the towns and villages and suburbs, in the middle-class congregations which (as a recent *Saturday Night* article puts it) feel alienated from an ecclesiastical leadership that is, or thinks itself, ethically *avant garde*.[5] As we ought to have learnt from Rudolf Bultmann, if we did not already learn it from St. Paul, the ethical 'imperative' presupposes a theological 'indicative'; or as the Reformers put it, the Law presupposes the Gospel. And if the leadership of the church has stinted in its efforts to help ordinary Christian people acquire a profound working awareness of the theological basis of the faith, and it has (!), then we should hardly be surprised if the ethical consequences of our own wrestling with Christ and culture are received by these same people as radical non sequiturs! If we have taught people—or allowed them to think—that the Christian Gospel is just a stained-glass version of the dominant Canadian virtues and values, then we should not expect them simply to acquiesce when, from our lecterns or our 'head offices' or our committees and councils we announce that the really *Christian* attitude to a whole host of things from sex to Sunday shopping is utterly discontinuous with prevailing social mores. At very least, the current furor over the ordination of self-acknowledged homosexual persons ought to alert us to the crying need in the churches for *serious theological* work.

But there is another side of all this which is more complex, and more difficult to articulate. I will state it therefore in the form of a series of questions: Have those of us who are vocationally responsible for stimulating the thought and action of the churches ourselves continued earnestly to wrestle with the fundamental basis of our belief? Have we perhaps simply assumed that we have completed our theological apprenticeship—treating the rudiments of our tradition as finger-exercises, enabling us now to play the real music? Have we become so absorbed in 'the issues' (they are after all very absorbing) that we have been tempted to think that they alone constitute our obligation as Christians? Have "justice, peace,

---

5 *The Uncomfortable Pulpit*, by Ivor Shapiro; May, 1988; pp. 23 f.

and the integrity of creation" (the present main theme of the World Council of Churches) assumed, as it were, the proportions of ultimacy, so that we feel no need to search, beyond them, in them, *under* them, for first causes or prime movers, for depths of estrangement or heights of redemption?

And let me become even more susceptible to criticism that may in some respects be justified - still it must be asked: Is it possible that absorption with 'the issues' functions for some of us, subtly, as *our* way of perpetuating Christendom, and so of avoiding the call to discipleship? There is, after all, something very heady about involvement in many of the issues that have (quite rightly!) claimed our attention and our service! Many of them are newsworthy items! And it is a heady thing for Christians, especially at a time of apparent disinterest in conventional religion, to find themselves featured in the media. Publicity, in a society narcissistically fixated on itself, can easily become the new form of power-questing in Christendom. And have we perhaps come dangerously near to a situation where orientation to any form of truth that does not end in being a 'media event' is no longer very interesting?

I ask these questions - I ask them of myself! - because I believe that the tradition in which we stand is one of enduring wisdom about eternal as well as temporal realities. This tradition provides us with a vantage-point from which to reflect on ultimate meaning, with a perspective from which to gain the courage (and much courage is required!) to enter the uncharted darkness of our historical moment, and with a language to name both the most insidious wickedness and the most noble ends to which human and creaturely existence can attain. We are not asked - by no means! - to cease devoting our best energies of mind and muscle to the understanding and alleviation of the great crises of our age, any one of which, or any combination, could destroy our civilization. This is no plea, on my part, to desist in our *doing* in order to fulfil our capacity for *thinking* and *praying!* But I feel certain that if we are not able (and better than we have been!) to *combine* deed and thought, law and gospel, ethic and theology, then we shall not have made good the gifts that belong to this community of "compassion and solidarity" (Baum). Christian mission today means the stewarding of life - of life itself - in death's kingdom; and therefore there is no alternative for us than to involve ourselves to the hilt in warding off the demonic forces of injustice, war, and creational disintegration. But life *is* more than food and the body more than raiment, and therefore *in* our devotion to the issues we must always seek to go . . . *beyond the issues*.

CONCLUSION

Beyond Christendom. Beyond Tolerance. Beyond Religious Simplism. Beyond the Issues. There are of course countless other barriers to the realization of the witnessing community that, with the demise of Christendom, the Church of Jesus Christ might become. I suppose we cannot even *see* many of these obstacles yet; we are still too near to Christendom. But whenever I encounter intimations of the church that has gone over, or begun to go over, into that future - as I do sometimes, in some of my students, in little movements here and there, in churches like those of Czechoslovakia and East Germany where Christendom was forcibly ended, in minorities within the Third and First Worlds too - whenever I experience these, directly or indirectly, I feel that it is true: the end of Christendom *could be* . . . a new beginning of the Church.

IV

FACING THE FUTURE: TRUST AND IMAGINATION

O God who has made us the creatures of time, so that every tomorrow is an unknown country, and every decision a venture of faith, grant us, frail children of the day, who are blind to the future, to move toward it with a sure confidence in your love, from which neither life nor death can separate us.

- Reinhold Niebuhr

INTRODUCTION:
ECCLESIASTICAL FUTURE SHOCK

Our concern throughout this discussion, even when we spoke about the past, has been the future of the church - the church as a whole, our denomination in particular, the congregations to which we belong and which we serve. Where are we going?

Clearly, Christians everywhere today are experiencing a moment of conspicuous change. We feel ourselves to be on the threshold of something new, different, largely unanticipated. For many of us it is an unnerving experience. Particularly is this so for members of confessional bodies whose commitment to the here-and-now has been more prominent than their desire merely to conserve intact their own past. In The United Church of Canada, which for this and other reasons has been more vulnerable to change than most of the Christian denominations in our country, some are so shaken by recent developments that they feel they must leave. They seek security in forms of the church more firmly anchored in convention, less exposed to 'the winds of change.' And most of the rest of us, who have no intention of abandoning this ship, who may even think that its passage has become surprisingly thought-provoking, still find ourselves wondering what sort of future we are entering. Will there *be* a United Church of Canada in fifty years? a hundred years?

Of course, if within a century The United Church of Canada were to disappear into a genuinely ecumenical Christian movement this would not disturb our peace; for precisely that has been from the outset the vision of this "uniting" church. In some sense to 'disappear,' to be absorbed into something more truly representative of the 'oneness' for which Jesus prayed [John 17:21] is our very charter! *Ut omnes unum sint.* What bothers us now, however, is the prospect of a disappearing act that cannot be justified on the basis of our union, or on the basis of any viable conception of Christ's Body. We fear that the whole vision could simply dissolve, if not through attrition, including the loss of members, then perhaps through the loss of any compelling 'reason to be,' - or, more accurately, of any reason to be *different*. Where *are* we going?

It will help to clarify, if not to dispell this ecclesiastical future shock if we consider it in the light of the general biblical perspective on the future. It is after all quite possible that *alarm* over the future of the church is only a species of the anxiety that has gripped our society at large as it contemplates the enormity of transition through which it is passing. How much of the apprehension that characterizes congregational life in these last decades of the 20th century is distinctively *Christian* concern? To what extent is it attributable, on the contrary, to mental and emotional attitudes to the future which are what they are precisely because they have lost touch with the orientation towards the future that is peculiar to the tradition of Jerusalem?

1. CHRISTIAN PERSPECTIVE ON THE FUTURE

Biblical faith manifests two attitudes towards the future - or, more precisely, a single outlook with two distinctive features. The two are related to one another in a rather paradoxical way - by which I mean that they seem, on the one hand, to contain a contradictory element, yet on the other it must be said that they condition and even support one another. In the end they produce a very arresting ethic - an odd but finally evocative combination of *great realism and a great protest against 'reality.'*

The first - and I think we must regard it as the dominant or foundational Christian attitude towards the future - is the one articulated in a beautiful and moving way in the prayer of Reinhold Niebuhr that I have set at the beginning of this final section. As creatures of time we do not know, *cannot* know the future. Every tomorrow is "an unknown country," every decision "a risk." The future is in *God's* hands. For our part, all that we can do is to *trust* God. But that is finally . . . enough!

> *God is our refuge and strength,*
> *a very present help in trouble.*
> *Therefore we will not fear though*
> *the earth should change,*
> *though the mountains shake in*
> *the heart of the sea;*
> *though its waters roar and foam,*
> *though the mountains tremble*
> *with its tumult.* [Psalm 46: 1-3]

If we trust God we shall not have *certitude* about the future, because certitude assumes a knowledge that we cannot possess. Certitude is in any case a category that does not belong to this faith-tradition. Certitude goes with "sight," and our Christian condition is not one of sight but of faith [Heb. 11:1; Rom. 8:24-25; I Cor. 13:12]. What belongs to faith in the biblical sense is precisely the term that Niebuhr employs in his prayer: "confidence." Trusting the God who is sovereign of the future as of the past, we we shall have *confidence* (from the Latin *con + fide* , i.e. 'with faith.') Having faith, not in ourselves, nor governments, nor systems, nor ideologies, nor even theologies and doctrines but *in God*, we shall be given the assurance that is needed to "move towards" the future that we do not know; because nothing that that future might contain - nothing! - " will be able to separate us from the love of God in Christ Jesus our Lord" [Romans 8:39].

This first and most basic biblical attitude towards the future, which applies as much to the life of the Christian *community* as to individual believers, could, however, without any further qualification lead to the sort of *resignation* that is *not* compatible with biblical faith. Granted, such resignation - amounting sometimes to plain fatalism - has frequently enough in Christian circles been mistaken for 'great faith.' After every accident, every natural disaster, one can hear pious souls murmuring that it was "the will of God." In the face of the terrible injustices which beset the human population of earth (every day 40,000 children die of hunger-related causes!) some good Christians will be heard to recite that "the poor you have always with you." And others will echo, in the presence of violence and war, that "wars and rumours of wars" constitute in any case the human condition - a logic which in an age of nuclearism leads them to conclude that 'it all has to end somewhere, anyway.'

Expressions of resignation may *on occasion* represent a genuine appropriation of trust in the God who "moves in mysterious way," but when they express, as they frequently do, a whole outlook on life they do not reflect biblical faith and obedience. Perhaps they reflect *Stoic* courage, which Paul Tillich judged to be the great rival faith of Christianity in the West;[1] but Christian

---

[1]   See Paul Tillich, *The Courage To Be* (New Haven: Yale University Press, 1952); pp. 9 ff.

74

courage is not the courage of unqualified *acceptance*. It is not a matter of saying 'Amen' to everything - "Whatever will be will be." Because the faith which trusts God in the face of whatever happens is also a faith which believes it has been given a definite *responsibility* for whatever happens [see Matthew 16:19!].

Nobody knew that better than did the writer of the prayer at the head of this chapter. You can detect this other, second thrust in the Judeo-Christian attitude towards the future (if you knew Niebuhr you couldn't avoid it!) in what the author says about having the confidence to "move towards" the unknown tomorrow. This confidence, we have emphasized already, is born of trust *in God*. It is a gift that goes "with" [*con*] faith [*fide*]. But the God who thus graciously fortifies our "frail" nature, in doing so instills in us a strength that otherwise we do not have - or think we do not have, or perhaps bungle because we imagine we already have it in abundance! The same faith which trusts this Other finds itself, in the act of trusting, endowed with the courage to believe that it could actually live up to the responsibility - the creaturely "dominion"[2] [Genesis 1:26-27] - that it has been commanded to assume. So it "moves towards" the future - not as one who is given extraordinary vision and knows everything in advance; nor on the other hand as one blindfolded and simply waiting for whatever the next step will bring, probably expecting the worst; but rather as one whose eyes are wide open, who is able to see a little way ahead, and *who therefore casts about for alternatives*.

In short, *A high degree of imagination is required of those who trust in God!*

---

[2]   I think that we should try to redeem this biblical word from its wrong connotations. So long as *God* is *Dominus*, there can be no question of human prometheanism! As I attempted to demonstrate in my book, *Imaging God: Dominion As Stewardship* (Grand Rapids: Wm. B. Eerdmans Publishing Co., 1986), what is intended by the (now controversial) word "dominion" in the creation saga and elsewhere (especially Psalm 8) is the vocation of *responsibility* that the human creature is called to assume, mirroring, *within* the creation, God's own compassionate care for all created life.

To be sure, one can only move 'ahead.' The laws of time do not permit of either standing still or moving backwards. That is why the attempt to recover Christendom and the 'living as if' responses to the humiliation of the church, which we considered in a previous section of this little document, are untenable. Christian realism means facing not only the actual data of our situation but also the necessity of moving on. Like the people of Israel at the edge of the Red Sea, we can't turn back; we have to keep going forward. But to go forward in faith, with confidence, means being on the lookout for alternative routes. Forward does not mean simply straightforward - 'walking the line,' so to speak, from one inevitability to the next. The ethic which flows from this confidence, we said, is an evocative combination of great realism and a great protest against 'reality.' It is realistic to obey the law of time: one must move forward. It is a protest against what usually passes for 'realism' to insist: there are, after all, *different ways of moving forward!* This is what the 'newcomers' in my Introduction knew and the old, established families did not, or would not.

It is not necessary to exaggerate here. The alternatives are not *infinite!* They are limited - sometimes frighteningly limited. Limited by our finitude, including our ignorance; limited by past events over which we have no control beyond the control of interpretation (which is however considerable!); limited by the needs and desires of others, human and extrahuman, with whom we share this small planet. But there *are* alternatives all the same. Even humanly speaking, quite apart from any mention of 'special grace,' there are usually fairly distinct choices in our movement from moment to moment, year to year, age to age.

But the confidence that belongs to faith is prepared to expect alternatives even when there are, humanly speaking, no alternatives left. Even when (as at the Red Sea's rim; as on the road to Emmaus!) the limits seem total, alternatives often open to us. Some of them are such that we could not even have *seen* them had we not first been deprived of the sorts of alternatives we had been accustomed to entertaining. It is in fact almost a law - certainly it is a recurring pattern - of the biblical narrative that 'the Way' opens to the community of trust only as *its* ways are blocked and *its* plans frustrated.

This pattern is classically expressed, for the church, in the "upper room" experience of the original disciple community [Acts 2]. One pictures the little remnant huddled in that place, distraught and discouraged, feeling they had come to the end of everything that they had dreamt of, having enough imagination left only to do what we so often do in the churches when we have no imagination left - hold a meeting; have an election of officers! And just at this point of failure and impossibility, the possibility is given for which everything leading up to it had been done: the Good News is heard, and proclaimed, and understood. The church is born.

The church would *not* have been born, however, had the original disciple community failed to discern and to seize the opportunity that had opened to it. We, piously, tend to assume that it was simply a matter of necessity - irresistible grace! And of course it was. But as both church history and our own individual histories amply illustrate, 'irresistible grace' is frequently and very successfully resisted! The disciples of Jesus were practiced in such resistence. If at this point - Pentecost - they at last broke their well-established habit of thwarting divine grace, it was surely not because they were simply overwhelmed, bound and gagged and conquered utterly by the creating Spirit. *Of course* it was only extraordinary grace that could break down such stubborn and (yes) almost stupid resistance as they are portrayed as having heretofore. But when once they *saw* the new possibility, they had to make it their own if it were to become what it could become. And we know from their continuing story, and from the story of the church throughout the ages, and from our own stories, that the process of

77

'making it their own' was by no means a once-for-all decision and act, but one which had to be taken over and over again, and in the face of the disciple community's continuing resistance and of its profound reluctance to walk 'the way of the Cross.'

When our eyes are opened to *God's* possibilities [Mark 10:27], we may discover within ourselves, as they did, enough trust to choose the way that wasn't there before, and enough imagination to make it a truly *viable* way. It is never an *easy* choice. It is after all always some variation on . . . 'the Way of the Cross.' But it is a way, an access to the future beyond the impasse of the present; and if we do not choose it when it presents itself to us, there is no guarantee that it will continue to be there.

There is thus a strange and never quite 'reasonable' interconnection between the recognition that God alone determines the future and that God makes us responsible for it. ". . . work out your own salvation with fear and trembling; for God is at work in you . . ." [Phil. 4:12]. The possibility of getting into the future beyond the cul-de-sac of the present is always a matter of "sheer grace" and "sheer faith" [*sola gratia, sola fide*]. But *obedience* to this possibility and necessity calls for decision and imagination. Even a thinker as convinced of sovereignty and providence of God as Karl Barth wrote passionately about this grace-given freedom/responsibility of the human creature: "We are not merely the pawn in a secondary theatre of action, but the responsible person on the spot at the very heart of things, the one who decides what creation is to become."[3]

In another and more famous of his prayers, Reinhold Niebuhr captured the essence of these two prongs of the biblical attitude towards the future, retaining the element of paradox within them and at the same time showing how essential they are one to another. (And in parentheses let me remark that those of us who are

---

3 *Church Dogmatics,* III/3; p. 234.

preachers and teachers within the church would do well to recognize that Niebuhr accomplished this theological subtlety in words that have become accessible and meaningful to thousands of people who have no theological education at all, many of whom would be properly astonished if they knew that the prayer they use daily (as alcoholics, for example) had been written by an erudite Christian academic!):

> *Give us the serenity to accept what cannot be changed,*
> *The courage to change what can be changed,*
> *And the wisdom to distinguish the one from the other.*

"Give us the serenity to accept . . . ." Acceptance is *part* of the gift of faith. It does not however lead to mute resignation. There are strong patterns and influences and inevitabilities whose external reality we cannot greatly alter (though there are certainly different ways of *internalizing* them). At the same time, there are things that "can be changed": we are not simply at the mercy of the momentum created by past decisions and actions, indecisions and inactions. Both the serenity of acceptance and the courage to change are gifts of the same grace that elicits faith in us; and *both* are expressions of the hope that is the future dimension of that faith. What is *always* needed (and it is undoubtedly always hard to come by!) is "the wisdom to distinguish the one from the other."

2. GOD IS FAITHFUL, WE ARE RESPONSIBLE

Applying this dual (dialectical) perspective on the future to our question about the future *of the church*, what might we derive by way of guidance?

Two overarching themes emerge in response to this question, corresponding to the two-sided outlook on the future that we have been considering. The *first* (and again I would insist, foundational) theme is that **while we cannot** *know* **what the future of the church will be, we can trust that God will be faithful.** *God* will be faithful, and therefore whatever is *essential* will not be lost.

But here we must pause and consider such an affirmation circumspectly. God's faithfulness, as it is repeatedly depicted in Scripture, certainly means that what is essential to the work of the community of faith and witness will not be lost. "... the powers of death shall not prevail against it" [Matt. 16:18 b]. But the same scriptural testimony makes it abundantly clear that what the 'people of God' at any given historical moment may *regard* as essential is not necessarily identical with what, in the divine wisdom, God apparently considers should withstand everything that strives to "prevail" against it. Indeed, much that ancient Israel and the earliest Christians clung to had to be discarded or allowed to atrophy - and precisely *in order that* what was essential could be preserved. The entire prophetic stream of Hebraic faith is epitomized in Jesus' refrain in the Sermon on the Mount, "You have heard that it was said of old. ... But I say to you ...." [Matthew 5]. Always, the 'essence' of the message and of the community of those who testified to it had to be distinguished from the 'accidental' elements with which, through association, they were equated.

That winnowing process, the separating of the wheat from the chaff, has continued throughout history; and we know that it cannot occur without pain! Because there is hardly an aspect of churchly existence that is not regarded by somebody as being 'of the essence!' Students of the history of the church will not be surprised if people cling to all kinds of things as though they were the very heart and soul of the Faith and the true 'marks of the Church', when in fact they are just historical accretions - sometimes vital for their time and place, sometimes incidental or trivial, sometimes obviously imported from non- or sub-Christian quarters.

Thus, to the Jerusalem disciples, Paul was endangering the

very core of the gospel when he determined that it should be proclaimed openly amongst the Gentiles [see Galatians Chapters 1 and 2]. To the Eastern Church, the West's introduction of the so-called *filioque* clause into the Nicene Creed was tampering with the faith once delivered to the prophets and apostles and saints and endangering the future of the Ecclesia![4] To hundreds of thousands of loyal Catholics at the time of the Reformation, almost *everything* essential to the Church's existence seemed to be jettisoned by Luther and his followers - not only the papacy but (what was far worse) a right understanding and practice of ministry and the sacraments, and therefore the very prospect of eternal salvation! To many of those same followers of Luther, the Anabaptists and other "enthusiasts" ("swarmers," Luther called them) were destroying the essence of the Church because they refused the long-established patterns of a concordat between church and state and chose rather to live outside 'the System.' And dare I mention, to bring the matter nearer home, that in 1925 many Canadian churchfolk felt that the displacement of a time-honoured doctrinal confession, or changes in this or that practice with regard to the character and duration of professional ministry, yes or the relinquishing of *buildings and properties*, or of psalms-in-meter, or the vocabulary of ecclesiastical polity, or of who knows what else constituted a veritable loss of the fabric of the church?

If one is not moved by the biblical theology of the future, this history alone ought to persuade one that what may appear to one age or 'province' of Christendom absolute, unalterable, the condition without which the church would not be the church, may to another seem purely relative, and even detrimental. Such an historical lesson does not give us licence arbitrarily to throw out this and that - whatever is no longer easily believable, whatever seems old-

---

[4] In 589 C.E., the Western Church at the Council of Toledo insisted that the Holy Spirit proceeds, not only "from the Father," as the original creed had affirmed, but "from the Father *and the Son*" [*ex Patre Filioque procedit*]

fashioned, etc. Christian modernists earlier in this century pursued that line, and in the long run it meant that they were indistinguishable from the sociological wallpaper! But history *does* instruct us, surely, that we have to be very thoughtful indeed about identifying 'the essence' of the church.

For instance, we need seriously to enquire today whether such things as a salaried full-time clergy, permanent and single-purpose buildings (sanctuaries), worship services mainly on Sundays, infant baptism, hymn-singing, and a whole host of other strongly entrenched conventions are really 'of the essence' - or even for the well-being (*bene esse*) of the church. If we say that they are, then we shall have to reckon with the fact that the first Christians (and many since) managed rather well without most of them! Would it imperil the very soul of the *koinonia* if pension plans and 'head offices,' housing allowances, car allowances, Christian education 'plants,' and all such undoubtedly convenient accoutrements of ecclesiastical life today were to be swept away by winds of change that are already blowing?

God will be faithful, and therefore though we do not *know* whether such things will in fact occur, or at least to what extent they will condition our future, we can have confidence that what is essential will remain.

The *second* theme that emerges from our reflections on faith's attitude towards the future as it applies to the future of the church is the theme of our *own responsibility for that future*. We are not thrown into a purely passive role. God is sovereign of the future, but God incorporates us into the sphere of that sovereign care. To put it in another way (as Paul did): "We are stewards of the mysteries of God" [I Cor. 4:1]. We do not *create* the alternatives that present themselves as possibilities for our life and witness as a disciple community; but both the *perception* and the *implementation* of these possibilities are within the purview of our freedom in serving the Christ.

Discipleship is first a matter of perception, discernment: the stewardship of wisdom - "the wisdom to distinguish" what must be accepted from what can and must be changed. A good deal of what will in fact come to pass in the church of the future depends upon our present ability and willingness as Christian congregations and persons to *perceive* the possibilities that are actually being offered us by divine providence already here and now.

Such perception is itself never painless. Earlier we remembered - with an allusion to the Red Sea and the Emmaus Road - that *seeing* alternatives frequently only occurs at the point of experiencing the loss of *familiar* alternatives. A way opens up when there seems no longer to be a way. Not only with the core events of the Exodus and the Resurrection, but again and again the biblical story illustrates how our human plans, schemes, expectations, desires, assumptions and the like must suffer frustration *in order that* we may be brought to a condition of real discernment. The 'eyes of faith' are opened, apparently, only when our usual apparatus for 'seeing' suffers a setback - the real point, surely, of Paul's 'Damascus Road' experience. The two on the Emmaus Road literally did not see how they could go on. The truth is, of course, that they *couldn't* go on - given their presuppositions concerning what Jesus was about and where he intended to take them! They had to have *that* perception dashed if they were going to be in a position to discern the Way that was actually being offered them.

It seems to me that many within the churches today are still on the road to Emmaus, dismayed and discouraged. For some it would be more appropriate to employ the Red Sea imagery: they stand at the edge of the future frustrated, annoyed, complaining. Both types lack discernment because they refuse to accept the impasse that they vaguely, or perhaps even clearly, sense. Still clinging to the 'great expectations' that fifteen centuries of Christendom have conditioned them to entertain, they do not discern the *hope* that is possible now - that is possible, in part, precisely because those kinds of expectations have been and are being set aside. They do not allow themselves to think that God is involved in the dashing of those great expectations and therefore they are also blind to the "hope against hope" [Romans 4:18] that enabled Abraham to "move towards" the unknown future. They can only see the humiliation of once-proud Christendom as a failure *on our part*: somewhere we went wrong; somewhere we followed the wrong path, the wrong leaders. Their imaginations are circumscribed, cramped, and ironically subservient to the patterns and conventions of Christendom, even while they criticize the failure of Christendom. Because they are constitutionally committed to the imperial model of the church, they cannot even *see* the possibilities of the church as a prophetic minority. Because they are committed to a stipended professional ministry they cannot even *see* the possibilities of tent-making ministries and the ministry of the laity. Because they are committed to this or that confessional posture or denominational identity, they cannot even *see* the prospect of a *global* Christianity which has transcended the past and risen to the challenge of our common planetary future. Because they are committed to a version of Christian truth which makes dialogue with other faiths *a priori* impossible, they cannot even *see* that such dialogue can enhance our comprehension of *our own faith* as well as open up worlds that are presently closed to us. Because they are committed to an ordained ministry that is exclusively or predominantly male, they cannot even *see* that women bring to the office of ministry in the church gifts that men do not and even cannot possess. Because they are committed to lifestyles that reproduce, at least externally, the dominant mores of the middle classes, they cannot even *see* that persons who deviate from these norms, whether by necessity or choice, are frequently more sensitive to human suffering than those whose conventional behaviour insulates them from much of the subtle pain of their social milieu.

Genuine trust in God elicits a lively imagination in those who trust. Often, those who constitute themselves 'conservers' of the past are simply deficient in both trust and imagination. Their carefully nurtured conventions of doctrine and practice function in much the same way as the blankets and toys and other objects carried by little children far beyond their cradle days. I should be the last to belittle the importance of tradition, and especially in ecclesiastical and social contexts like our own where both awareness of and respect for Christian tradition is thin. But if we give ourselves *seriously* to the contemplation of our long Judeo-Christian heritage, and are not just *using* 'tradition' to justify our own preconceived notions and vested interests, we shall find that it upholds in the most decisive way the thesis advanced in the first sentence of this paragraph - that trust in God begets an inspired imagination. What *is* this tradition, this rich and varied history that has been 'handed over' [*tradere*] to us, if it is not the imaginative working out of the meaning of 'gospel' on the part of human spirits sufficiently trustful of God to risk novelty and change, new interpretations of the past and new ventures for the future? *That* is what we must conserve! In that we must all be conservatives!

Today, at the end of "the Constantinian era," unheard-of opportunities are being given a disciple community that is ready to become part of that tradition of trust and imagination. These opportunities are accessible, however, *only* to Christian communities that can appropriate a sufficient confidence in *God's* capacity to sustain what is essential to Christian existence and witness that they are able to imagine and to implement new expressions of the church and every aspect of the Christian life. Such communities will by no means belittle the past, with its accumulated wisdom. On the contrary, because they are in dead earnest about finding a way into the future, they will pay more real attention to the past than those who turn the past - some past, real or imagined - into their reason for existing. Because they shall need all the help they can get, such communities of trust and imagination will devote themselves to an unearthing of the tradition in all of its plenitude - as indeed feminists and liberationists and others are doing today.

They will not be content with learning the tradition from those who have set themselves up as its guardians, but will go in for original investigation, uncovering what was buried by the powerful conventions of evolving Christendom and discovering submerged and minority traditions which may have been *more faithful* to the primitive, biblical past of the Christian movement but were pushed aside by the demands of imperial religion, patriarchal ministry, intellectual 'respectability,' class conformity, and all the accoutrements of Establishment.

In their search for "a usable past", however, such communities of trust and imagination will be guided by one thing: the compulsion of faith to be obedient *now* and *here*. The past elicits their respect, but it is the present and impending future that demands their responsibility. They can safely leave ultimate significance and preservation of the past to God. What God requires of them is that they work out a faithful Christian *praxis* for the context in which they now live. Their real continuity with the great tradition will only materialize as they, like the sages and saints and martyrs of our history, allow themselves to become the cutting edge of a movement that is "always re-forming" [*semper reformanda*] itself to meet the demands of the gospel. What is truly 'gospel' ("good news") only emerges in relation to the "bad news" that Time continuously introduces. With an incarnational faith, the message that is brought forward and enacted by the community of belief will be shaped and reshaped by the ever-changing realities of the world; and the community itself will always have to re-form itself if it is to keep pace with the message - the living Word - to which it is called to bear witness. The Church of Jesus Christ will only lose its essence - its "soul," its "life" [Matt. 10:39] - if it allows the desire to *save itself* to prevent its being re-formed by the creating Spirit for the sake of the mission with which it is entrusted.

3.   THE ESSENTIALS

But what is its essence? God is faithful, we have said, and will preserve the essence of the church. We have also insisted that this essence is not to be identified lightly. It cannot be equated with whatever, at any given historical moment, ecclesiastical opinion regards as being indispensable. But can it be defined at all? Is every definition bound to exalt the bias of the times and of its authorship? Are we abandoned to unrelieved uncertainty here? Or, what is worse, to the all-too-certain explanations of factions and strong personalities within the community who are always prepared to tell us precisely what the 'true church' is?

At the end of his learned and influencial work, *Christianity and History*,[5] Herbert Butterfield, surveying the mood of his age, concluded that

> Christianity is not tied to regimes - not compelled to regard the existing order as the very end of life and the embodiment of all our values. Christians have too often tried to put the brake on things in the past, but at the critical turning-points in history they have less reason than others to be afraid that a new kind of society or civilization will leave them with nothing to live for. . . .There are times when we can never meet the future with sufficient elasticity of mind, especially if we are locked in the contemporary systems of thought. We can do worse than remember a principle which both gives us a firm Rock and leaves us the maximum elasticity for our minds: the principle: *Hold to Christ, and for the rest be totally uncommitted.*

The advice of the great Cambridge historian is still pertinent, or perhaps *newly* pertinent as, forty years later, we begin to realize that the "regimes" to which the Christian movement has been tied consist not only of specific nations and empires and class-systems of the Western world but of that 'Christendom' which for sixteen hundred years has shaped and been shaped by them all. At the

[5]   New York: Charles Scribner's Sons, 1949-1950; p. 146. [My italics].

waning of Christendom, when the great temptation of Christians is to preserve intact as much of the residue of Christendom as can be salvaged, it is singularly instructive to contemplate the principle, "Hold to Christ, and for the rest be totally uncommitted." The note that is sounded here is, once again, that *foundational* one, the great major chord of Christian hope: that God will be faithful, come what may; that the Church of Jesus Christ will be wherever, implicitly or explicitly, there is *trust* in that God.

In a real sense, it is not possible to surpass that indication of the essence of the church. The very first intimations of the reality of the church occurred precisely at that point when a human being recognized, in the person of Jesus, the Christ who was God's fulfilment of the promise of faithfulness, the consummation of God's determination not to abandon this world. "Thou art the Christ . . . . " [Matthew 16:16]. Wherever this confession is found - and found as *confession*, not merely as *profession!* - there will the church be found, though it may not always be conscious of itself as such [Matthew 25:31 ff.].

Where the confession is intentional, however, this 'holding to Christ' will incorporate a number of secondary or penultimate characteristics through which it will express its confession and profession of faith. It seems to me important to stress that these are *penultimate*, and by that I mean (i) that they must never be elevated to the status of absolutes ("Hold to *Christ!* "), (ii) that they should not be strictly circumscribed in the way that the four traditional *notae ecclesae* ['marks of the church'], conventionally exegeted, can too easily imply, and (iii) that no historical exposition of them should become so fixed and inflexible that they are virtually incapable of engaging the real situation of the community of witness.

With these qualifications, we may nevertheless still find in the traditional 'marks of the church' ways of identifying for our own context what would have to remain if the church of the future, for which we are now preparing, were faithfully to manifest the trust and imagination about which we have been thinking. The four 'marks,' stemming from the Nicene Creed's article on the Church ("one, holy, catholic and apostolic") at least provide a framework for reflecting upon the church's "essence;" and if we can in this way demonstrate something of the manner in which the disciple community is called to wrest its present confession and self-understanding from an ongoing dialogue with the tradition, so much the better.

(i)   *Unity:*

To "hold to Christ" means to be committed to a process and quest for reconciliation and mutuality that is literally unlimited. Not only did Jesus, according to John's interpretation, pray "that all may be one," but the whole thrust of the story that is told in the continuity of the Testaments concerns the reuniting of that which, through human and supra-human distortion, has been divided and estranged - a reuniting which does not destroy but positively upholds the distinctiveness of each participant.

This has always been recognized by the most responsible representatives of the Christian faith throughout the centuries, and the many-faceted 'ecumenical movement' of our own century is in a real way the culmination of this recognition. All the metaphors of the church in the newer Testament assume 'oneness': the Body, the Bride of Christ, the Vine and its branches, etc. A church which rejected this implication of the 'at-one-ing' Word of the Cross would be a contradiction in terms. A church which, while not actively resisting the unity principle, was nevertheless content to live its own life in isolation from other 'separated' brothers and sisters, fostering its own 'denominational' enterprises, sustaining its own independent mission, assuming the rectitude and plenitude of its own forms of ministry, worship, and mission and never asking seriously whether such priorities were proper to disciples of Jesus Christ: such a church would also, surely, beg the question of its own authenticity.

The first imperative, therefore, which issues from the mark of unity for a church seeking its way into the future is that *ecumenicity is today not just an option, it is the **minimal** requirement of serious discipleship*. It is not enough for the churches of the world to lament "our tragic divisions;" these divisions are certainly amongst the things that *can be changed*. We do not have to accept them "with serenity". They are neither necessary nor inevitable. Besides being luxuries that a diminishing Christendom can no longer afford, they are living evidence of our lack of integrity and obedience. If the church of the future (and I do not mean the *distant* future) has not gone far beyond our present state of ecumenical inertia towards a more visible appropriation of the unity that the gospel *makes possible*, then something very questionable about our present pursuits as Christians will have been made shamefully plain![6]

While the mark of unity applies, traditionally, to the state of the church itself, it should also be regarded as part of the church's vision for God's beloved world. Today, no concern for *Christian* unity can be taken seriously unless it is part of this larger vision. Indeed, *if* the future demonstrates a new seriousness about Christian ecumenicity it will be, I suspect, because the churches have recognized that their own quest for ecclesiastical reunification is nothing more than a token of, and a means to, a much more expansive expression of the "oneness" for which the High Priest of Gethsemane was praying. Is not our lack of earnestness about our "tragic divisions" in fact due to our failure to perceive our own

[6] Albert van den Heuvel registers the shame that is already plain enough in this respect when, in his essay on "The Humiliation of the Church," he writes: "It is a scandal to see the beautiful ecumenical documents which the churches drew up together far away from the place where God had set them and which were never applied at home. If somebody has sufficient courage to make a study of cynicism, he should buy the reports of all major ecumenical gatherings, read them, and see what the churches said together. Then he should go to the balcony of his house and look over his city at the churches that are standing there, from which steeples have risen to heaven since the Middle Ages, and see how nothing has happened to them." (*Op.cit.*, p. 51).

ecclesiastical unity as *token* and *means*? Our silly, organizational enthusiasm over the little, frequently aborted mergers and 'dialogues' on which we have expended so much money and energy is hardly worthy of the name "ecumenical movement." What we need is precisely to have the matter of our own unification as churches put in its place by the greater need of the human and extrahuman creation that is crying out ["groaning in travail"—Rom. 8:22] for exactly some profound recognition and enactment of our common creaturehood.

Concretely this means at least two things: first, that the unity sought by God in Jesus Christ requires of those who profess it today and tomorrow an unconditional reaching out to other human beings and communities, especially to those who profess religious belief of any kind, but ultimately to *all* humanity. An ecumenicity which explicitly or implicitly *excludes* other faith traditions can only be seen, in our pluralistic world, as an anomaly or an anachronism - a vestige of imperial Christianity. A church which confesses the unity of God and of truth, yet fails to make deliberate overtures of reconciliation to all in whom the impulse to transcendence and the orientation to truth are present is theologically offensive and ethically culpable. As I trust I have demonstrated in the foregoing, the God of the Scriptures does not seem to me to be out to turn everybody into professing Christians (that is the god of Christendom!); but this God is certainly intent upon achieving universal reconciliation. In that sense, not in the sense of militant Christian expansionism, the Christian doctrine of redemption is universalist in nature.

But, secondly, the mark of unity could only be found in the Christian community today if it betokened, as well as a sense of universal *human* reconciliation, the desire on the part of the disciple community to exist as a means of making good the *de facto* unity of *all* the creatures of God. In an age of ecological disaster and impending catastrophe, a church which confined its unity principle to *human* mutuality and solidarity would indeed be lacking in imagination. Not only the creation sagas, especially the earliest [Genesis 2] with its creatures all made of common clay; and not only the eschatological vision of the reunification of all divided beings [e.g. Ephesians 1:10]; but also the whole history of redemption incorporates this concern of the tradition of Jerusalem for *the totality*. Nothing is more abhorrent to the best scriptural and traditional testimonies to the unity Christ seeks than is a 'Christianity' which rhapsodizes about the salvation of a few human beings without even considering, apparently, whether these "raptured" few have been snatched from the burning, not only of many others of their own kind, but also of . . . "much cattle" [Jonah 4:11]![7]

In short, the mark of "unity" may have more to say to us about the 'true church' than has been dreamt of in our theologies until now.

(ii) *Holiness:*

It is difficult to speak about holiness without conjuring up all sorts of images that in fact betray the tradition of Jerusalem, with its great earthiness and its celebration of creaturely existence. Holiness in the popular imagination (and well beyond the merely *popular* imagination!) connotes an otherworldliness that is either naively innocent of the real world or haughtily disparaging of ordinary finitude. The pejorative use of the adjective 'holy' almost makes it unfit for use in connection with an attempt to delineate the essence of the church. Even in the churches, people do not like to have this term applied to themselves.

---

[7]   It is an indication of the wisdom that is still possible in ecumenical Christianity today that the World Council of Churches, meeting in Vancouver in 1983, elected as its theme and its vocation for the ensuing years the task of engaging the churches in "mutual commitment" for "Justice, Peace, and the Integrity of Creation." This motif, around which the whole work of the Council now revolves, incorporates precisely the kind of concern for the *whole* creation that I have in mind here, and it does so in such a way that all others of good will who have "the fate of the earth" at heart can join Christians in this endeavour without feeling excluded by the very language adopted.

Whether or not the term as such is used, however, what it stood for in classical Christian parlance must not be lost. There are two, inter-related meanings: (1) the holy is that which is set apart, (2) holiness refers to a dimension of transcendence and mystery.

When it is claimed that holiness is a mark of the church, both of these meanings are implied. The church is 'set apart' from the world as a community called to hear, in the world's behalf, the Word of God. This was the special emphasis of Karl Barth, and it is entirely pertinent to our present context:

> The term 'holy' applied to the Church, to God's work, and to believers has then no direct moral meaning. It does not mean that these people are particularly suited to come near to God, to deserve his revelation, that these things are particularly adapted to represent God. Rather, holiness is conferred upon them as a matter of the fact that God has chosen them, both men and things, in order to reveal himself to them."[8]

Such an observation is, I say, pertinent to our situation, because the winnowing process that is presently dispersing the Christian "culture religion" (Berger) *could* be seen as the occasion for a new appropriation, in what remains of the church, of its holiness in this sense of the term: that is, that it is being distinguished from its host cultures precisely in order that it may act within these societies as a prophetic minority - salt, yeast, light, seed. So long as the church is merely part of the social mix, the "religious aspect," it is difficult for it to represent anything to and within the world that is not already part of it.

Along these lines, the church's *holiness* is the condition necessary to its witness to divine *justice*. *God's* justice, not just conformity to the code of decency or to an ideal, but to the command of the One who has "a preferential option for the poor," - that is, to those who *never are* part of the establishment, *any*

---

[8] *The Faith of the Church*, trans. by Gabriel Vahanian (New York: Living Age Books, published by Meridian Books, Inc., 1958), p. 138.

establishment.

This point is made forcibly by Gustavo Gutierrez in his commentary on the second general conference of Latin American bishops at Medellin:

> The denunciation of injustice [which is "the prevailing theme in the texts of the Latin American Church"] implies the rejection of the use of Christianity to legitimize the established order. It likewise implies, in fact, that the Church has entered into conflict with those who wield power. And finally it leads to acknowledging *the need for the separation of Church and state because 'this is of primary importance in liberating the Church from temporal ties and from the image projected by its bonds with the powerful. This separation will free the Church from compromising commitments and make it more able to speak out. It will show that in order to fulfill its mission, the Church relies more on the strength of the Lord than on the strength of Power.* . . .[9]

In short, the holiness of the Church is the basis of its deepest ethical (as distinct from merely 'moral') commitment to the life of the world.

But holiness has a second and related connotation that is equally relevant to our context: it refers to the reality of transcendence and mystery of which the church is conscious, not only in its own life but also in the life of the world. If Karl Barth has reminded us of the first connotation of holiness, Paul Tillich has taught us not to neglect the second:

> If in religion the great is called the holy, this indicates that religion is based on the manifestation of the holy itself, the divine ground of being. . . . In this sense one can speak of Holy Scriptures, holy communities, holy acts, holy offices, holy persons. These predicates mean that all these realities are more than they are in their immediate finite appearance. They are self-transcendent, or, seen from the side of that to which they

---

[9] *A Theology of Liberation*, trans. by Sister Caridad Inda and John Eagleson (Maryknoll, N.Y.: Orbis Books, 1973), p. 115. [My italics].

transcend - the holy - they are translucent toward it. This holiness is not their moral or cognitive or even religious quality but their power of pointing beyond themselves.[10]

The church of the present and impending future will have to manifest far more sensitivity towards 'the holy' in this sense than has most of the official Christianity of the past, particularly the Modern past, and more particularly modern Protestantism. Protestantism in contemporary North America still seems incapable, by and large, of transcending the ubiquitous one-dimensionality of the secular society. I have illustrated this at several points in the earlier parts of this text. The average church service smacks more of a performance than of 'divine service.' Few, I suspect, could ever derive from their attendance of the folksy, busy, chatty Sunday services that typify the majority of our 'mainline' denominations anything approaching a sense of wonder at the grandeur, terror, and utter giftedness of life - the *mysterium tremendum et fascinans*. Yet in a technocratic society where everything is 'known,' everything manipulable, and nothing sacred, the human spirit longs for nothing so much as for some intimation of the depth and mystery of existence ("I do not know how man can do without God"[11]). If the human spirit in its post-Modern, post-secular frustration does not find a correlate for its new quest for 'spirituality' in the religious institutions readily available to it, it will create its own media for the fulfilment of this quest - horoscopes, crystals, rock festivals, and also outlets less innocent than these!

In a real sense, I think, one way of stating the whole challenge confronting Christianity as it tries to find a way into the future is whether it can recover any sense of the holy, and in both of the above meanings. Isn't it possible that the *moralism* unfortunately associated with 'holiness' in the public mind is due primarily to our paucity of imagination in this entire area? Moralistic 'separate-

[10] *Systematic Theology*, Vol. III (Chicago: The University of Chicago Press, 1963), p. 99.

[11] Margaret Drabble, *The Ice Age, Op.cit.*, p.258; see the 'Introduction,' p. ii.

ness' ("holier-than-thou") and churchy pomposity, whether of the formal or allegedly informal variety, are no substitutes for prophetic justice and the profound awareness that our lives are more than they appear to be. During the course of this century, we have seen enough of the lostness and wickedness that transpires when human beings and societies have no operative sense of the transcendent mystery and "grandeur" (Pascal) of existence to realize the truth of what the great American scientist, Loren Eiseley wrote:

> Man is not as other creatures and . . . without the sense of the holy, without compassion, his brain can become a gray stalking horror - the deviser of Belsen.[12]

Unless the church can become in a genuine way 'sanctuary' - that is, to quote the splendid definition of a contemporary philosopher, a place "in which we are awed by the world"[13] - it will only function to corroborate the fundamental assumptions of a disillusioned secularity, namely that, the rhetoric notwithstanding, "We *are* ... alone."

(iii) *Catholicity:*

Hopefully by now, after so much discussion of this historically complicated term, all of those who will read these words will have digested the truth that 'catholic' means 'universal,' and is not a crypto-Roman or high-Anglican claim which we Protestants are tricked into confessing whenever (and *if* ever!) we are called upon to recite either of the historic creeds (for it is there in the Apostles' as well as the later Nicene Creed). To believe "the holy, *catholic* church"[14] means to understand the essence of the church to include its *universal* character. This has both negative and positive conno-

---

12 Quoted by Richard E. Wentz, "The American Spirituality of Loren Eiseley," in *The Christian Century*, April 25, 1984; p. 430.

13 Henryk Skolimowski, *Eco-Philosophy: Designing New Tactics for Living* (New York and London: Marion Boyars, 1981), p. 55.

14 Karl Barth (rightly, in my opinion) cautions that we do not believe "in" the church, but only "in" the Holy Spirit who is the church's creator (See , e.g., *Dogmatics In Outline*, trans. by G.T. Thomson; New York: Harper & Row, Publishers, 1959; pp. 141 ff.)

tations which are particularly cogent for today.

Negatively speaking, to confess that universality is one of the *notae ecclesae* - a characteristic without which the church would not be the church - is to *deny* that the church belongs to any one culture, nation, people, race, gender, class, historical confederacy, hemisphere, or 'world.' And this is an especially significant recognition, which must be brought home in particular to those historic and geographic groupings in the contemporary global community which have for so long seemed virtually to "own" the church! There are tensions today - and they are practically palpable in every ecumenical gathering - between the old established churches of the First and Second Worlds and the newer churches of the Third World; moreover, these tensions become more conspicuous as the latter bodies grow stronger and more numerous than the former - a trend which by all current predictions will increase dramatically in the future.

A similar, though yet more complex discomfort exists between the (still!) largely middle-class male-dominated hierarchies of the denominations of Christendom and Christian minorities, especially women and minorities based on race, economics, sexual orientation, etc. The sense of 'ownership' on the part of the former becomes all the more insidious (and occasionally virulent) as it feels itself challenged by those who, formerly, were content to leave to it the great decisions and actions of the church in all phases of its life.

In "the last days of the Constantinian era," there is a new opportunity - for all who exemplify the trust and imagination which are the main themes of this concluding essay - to discover concretely what 'catholicity' means. The church does not belong to any supposedly privileged group. It is there for *all* who hear and are drawn to the gospel, and no one has any 'right' to membership and leadership within the Christian community because of the accidents of birth! We 'belong' in the church solely and simply because of the grace of God. Our membership in other groups and organizations may (and usually is) the consequence of some qualification that *we* bring, or that others grant us - often, condescendingly. But the divine Spirit alone creates (*ex nihilo!*) the Church (which is why, in the Apostles' Creed, the confession of belief in the Holy Spirit immediately precedes the reference to "the holy, catholic church"). God alone grants our membership in the Body of Christ, and God "shows no partiality" [Gal. 2:6]. (The matter was put succinctly by a woman who, feeling implicitly that her full membership in a Christian congregation was being querried by some present, asserted: "I am in the university by the grace of some rather self-important people who decided that I was sufficiently educated and had published enough. I am in the church because of the grace of God - as are all the rest of you!")

Like all the other marks of the church, its catholicity is a matter of becoming, not an accomplished reality. At depth, it is predicated upon the reconciliation being accomplished through the work of the triune God - the creation of a global community in which "there cannot be Greek and Jew, circumcised and uncircumcised, barbarian, Scythian, slave, free person, but Christ is all, and in all." [Col. 3:11]. The end (*telos*) of this process, to which the church can point but which it cannot embody, is the 'Kingdom' - the Reign of God. No church can ever legitimately claim, therefore, to *be* "catholic;" but every church exists under the law that is within the gospel to allow the catholic (universal, ecumenical) thrust and impulse of that gospel to realize itself within its life and work in the world.

A particular aspect of this 'thrust and impulse' which will have to become a priority within the next decades is the necessity of working at a *global theology*. Since the end of World War II, *contextual* theologies have been evolving in many parts of the ecumenical church, and this must be regarded as one of the most hopeful signs of the emerging Christian movement. But at the same time it signals the need for a new appropriation of the 'catholic' essence of the Faith; for there is a certain danger that intensely contextualized versions of Christian belief and praxis, vital as they are to the Christian future, will court the sort of 'Babel' in which different 'provinces' of the universal church will not be able to understand one another any longer. There are already some disturbing indications of this, not only among theological communities working in three different 'worlds,' but also among differing orientations within each of those worlds. The new ecumenism that must follow from any imaginative appropriation of the mark of 'catholicism,' will not have as its object the reunion of divided denominations of Christendom so much as the quest for mutuality of understanding and communion between those who (quite rightly!) pursue the meaning and ethical implications of the gospel for their very different contexts. The more contextualized faith and theology become, the more important is it to offset the danger of parochialism through the nurture of a truly *global* ecumenical dialogue.

(iv) *Apostolicity:*

As with the mark of catholicism, so that of apostolicity contains two distinct though related implications. One of them - historically the most prominent - has to do with the necessary continuity of the 'true church' with the tradition of the apostles. The second implication, which has not claimed the attention of the church as consistently as it should have, is related to the meaning of the word 'apostle' itself (*apo* + *stellein* = to send forth). The two connotations are joined by a single thought: the church exists for the sake of the message that it bears, namely the message entrusted to the original apostles, which must continually be proclaimed by new messengers.

The Christian message is not just whatever anyone decides, one morning, that it should be! We are the inheritors of a tradition. We do not spin 'the gospel' out of our own entelechy. This in no way suggests that our personal, generational, racial, national, etc. experience is unimportant. Far from it. What has been 'handed over' has to be appropriated, and we can only appropriate it *as* we are, and when, and where. Besides, 'the message' would not even achieve its own intrinsic aim if it were simply transmitted and imbibed, swallowed whole! Surely this point has been secured in the foregoing.

But the danger that 'the message' *will be* whatever this or that individual, generation, or human grouping determines that it *should* be is a danger that has been present in the church from the beginning, and it is not lessened today but, if anything, more potent. The relegation of 'objectivity' to the exact sciences, along with the individualism and psychologism rampant in our epoch and aided by the breakdown of conventional forms of authority in the church: all this, and more, has produced a situation in which 'Christianity' is fair game for any who announce themselves as Christians. Nowhere is this more pathetically observable than in North America, with its (how many, perhaps 4000?) different 'denominations.'

The author of Ephesians [2:20] tells his non-Jewish congregation ("you Gentiles", [2:11, 3:1]) that it has been "built upon the foundation of apostles and prophets, Christ Jesus himself being the chief cornerstone, in whom the whole structure is joined together and grows into a holy temple in the Lord. . . ." This key text in the evolution of the church's consciousness of its 'apostolicity' is still timely, perhaps more timely today than ever before. A Christianity which, "after Auschwitz," attempts to discover its authentic roots and lineage must develop a working recognition that its 'apostolicity' joins the church indelibly to the *whole* tradition - not only the newer testamental tradition of 'the Twelve,' but that tradition which the original apostles themselves "searched daily" [Acts 17:11]. That 'apostolicity' contains also "the prophets" has hardly ever been taken with the strict theological and practical seriousness that it requires, despite the early church's rejection of Marcionism.

The influence of hellenistic and other philosophic and religious systems, together with the all-too-early Establishment of the Christian religion, meant that an effective separation of the church and the synagogue would prevent the Christian movement from ever exploring in depth the mystery of their inter-relatedness as discussed by Paul, for instance, in Romans, chapters 9 to 11. Not only for the sake of comprehending its role in the Holocaust, but for the sake of discovering a truly "usable past", the church today and tomorrow will have to manifest a profound concern for the recovery of 'apostolicity' in its fulness - namely, an apostolicity which includes the community of Israel, and centrally so.

The development of apostolic consciousness, as is well known, grew in proportion to the danger of uncontrolled diversification and what was felt to be heterodox opinion in the early centuries of the Christian movement. Eventually - inevitably? - it expressed itself in the concept and practice of "apostolic succession," the logic being that a duly recognized succession of ecclesial authorities (bishops) would guarantee, or at least support, the continuity of advancing Christianity with its own true past.

This raises the knotty question of the nature of ecclesiastical authority. Will the church of the future resort to stronger forms of ecclesial authority in order to safeguard the Faith? There can be no doubt that in the diaspora situation, where the Christian community has fewer ties with the official culture and where it is in dialogue with many other faith-options, there will be - as there was in the beginning! - a greater danger of the proliferation of many versions of 'the message' and many forms of the 'ambassadorial' community [2 Cor. 5:20]. It is today already a question whether, given the bureaucratization of churches and the breakdown of *effective* conciliar forms of government (e.g. presbyteries), 'free' churches like The United Church of Canada ought to opt at last for bishops (perhaps, after the pattern of our sister-communion in the U.S.A., the United Church of Christ, using the nomenclature "conference minister").

Whatever may be the outcome of such questions, what needs above all to be borne in mind is that the ecclesial offices exist for the perpetuation of 'the tradition,' and not for their own sake. Apostolic *Succession* was instituted in order to preserve the continuity of the Apostolic *Tradition* - not, as it has so characteristically appeared in the history of Christendom, as a device on whose basis the church would mimic (and outdo!) the hierarchic authority systems of empire! What is important - of 'the essence' - is not the papacy, the episcopacy, the three-fold form of ministry, or any of the other schemes adopted by evolving Christendom to meet its various needs and problems in this area, but that 'the message' should be kept in recognizable agreement with its foundational expressions.

The *second* implication of apostolicity, already contained in the first, is that this 'message' is ever in need of finding new voices to announce it. The 'apostle' is one "sent forth," not aimlessly but with a definite purpose, a mission. The apostolic community is a messenger-community.

There are a number of connotations here for any discussion of the question, "Where are we going?" One of them is that, wherever we think we are going, we shall have to remember that our purpose in going there is to be bearers of a message that transcends our own being - that is greater than 'churches,' and is intended for . . . "all" [Rom. 11:32][15]

It will not be necessary at this juncture to caution that the apostolic inclusiveness of the message announced by the community that is sent forth should not be translated forthwith into the categories and assumptions of imperial Christianity. That the gospel is intended for all does not mean that all are intended for the Church! But it does mean that the vocation of the church is a *public*

[15] See in this connection Karl Barth's splendid sermon of 22 September 1957, based on this text and entitled simply, "All!" *Deliverance to the Captives* (New York: Harper and Row, 1961/1978), pp. 85-92.

vocation. And that is a particularly needful lesson for Christian communities that will in future become "little flocks here and there" (Karl Rahner); for surely the *great* temptation of these communities will be to become very private, and thus to forget that, however small, or however peripheral in relation to the dominant cultures of their societies they may be, what they are obliged to stand for in the world is a Word that is addressed to the *world*.

It is a false assumption, though a common one, that a disestablished faith can no longer be a public faith. There is on the contrary every reason to believe that a church which is no longer part of the establishment can be of *far more use to the world as a whole than one which for centuries cast its lot with the powerful ones of the world.* Certainly its influence in society will be of a different sort: normally, it will qualify the life of the larger unity (the "loaf"), not from the top down but from the bottom up - i.e. from a posture of solidarity with the other disenfranchised ones with whom, in its new role, it is thrown together. It will not be chaplain to the court of the King, and *therefore* it may be constructive critic ("prophet") outside the halls of power. It will not be able to command a hearing because of its robes of office and its 'standing,' but it may be able to *earn* a hearing on account of its understanding, its wisdom.

In other words, let it be made entirely plain that in all of this discussion about the "humiliation of the church" we have not been opting for private religion. That the church is 'apostolic,' and that to retain its essence it must continue to be apostolic, means that it has a message for the world. That message, so far as its concrete articulation is concerned, will depend always upon what is actually 'going on' in the world, i.e. the explicit context, in which the witnessing community finds itself. At *base*, however, it is just this - that the church knows something about the world that, for the most part, the world does not know about itself: *that it is greatly loved.*

CONCLUSION: ON WEARING
THE COLOURS OF THE COURT

There is one other 'mark of the church' that does not appear explicitly in either of the historic confessions, though it is prominent in the Bible - in fact, the newer Testament has more to say about this than about any other single ecclesiastical theme: the *suffering* of the church. Luther made it so essential a mark of the true church that without it, he insisted, all the traditional marks would be rendered null and void:

> The holy, Christian Church is outwardly known by the holy possession of the Holy Cross. It must endure all hardship and persecution, all kinds of temptation and evil (as the Lord's Prayer says) from devil, world, and flesh; it must be inwardly sad, timid, terrified; outwardly poor, despised, sick, weak; thus it becomes like its head, Christ. The reason must be only this, - that it holds fast to Christ and God's Word and thus suffers for Christ's sake, according to Matthew 5 ... [16]

Drawing on the imagery of the medieval court, the Reformer puts the matter in a nutshell: "... if I want to be a Christian, I must also wear the colours of the court; the dear Christ issues no others in his court; suffering there must be."[17]

The suffering of the church is not to be equated with everything that causes us anguish, and it should not be something actually sought out by the Christian community; indeed, says Luther, "... it should be the kind of suffering which we have not chosen ourselves. ... It should be the kind of suffering which, if it were possible, we would gladly be rid of...!"[18] Jürgen Moltmann makes the same point in the opening sentence of his important study

[16] Hugh Thomson Kerr, *A Compend of Luther's Theology* (Philadelphia: The Westminster Press, 1943), p. 130 f.

[17] *Luther's Works*, Vol. 51, *Sermons*, trans. by John W. Doberstein (Philadelphia: Muhlenberg Press, 1959); p. 199.

[18] *Ibid.*, p. 198.

of the "theology of the cross," *The Crucified God*: "The cross is not and cannot be loved."[19] This suffering has nothing to do, in other words, with masochism and martyr-complexes.

What then is its rationale? Why is *this* mark of the church indispensable? Quite simply because suffering is the condition of God's beloved world, and therefore also of the God who loves it - the "crucified God." To wear the colours of the court of this God means to participate in the "divine pathos" (Heschel), the *passio Christi* [passion of the Christ]. To love, in some penetrating and tangible way, a suffering world is to be involved in *its* suffering.

> It is the way the Master went,
> Should not the servant tread it still?

In our Canadian churches we have known little of this suffering - though there are, as always, the . . . exceptions. The general ethos of our religious life has been, if not "the comfortable pew" (Pierre Burton), a certain basic satisfaction with the order of things. Our style of Christendom has had - as I tried to convey in the first lecture - its advantages, its laudable aspects and benefits. We have managed, on the whole, to avoid the excesses of fanaticism and the awesome waves of 'true belief' that have racked the soul of our more demonstrative neighbour to the south. A feeling of good will and broad social concern, born perhaps of our corporate Canadian realization that our survival over against harsh realities of both nature and history depended upon it, has never been far from congregational life in this country. Despite the gnawing suspicion that we are not a very colourful people and our usually erratic attempts to rectify this flaw, we Canadians think ourselves fairly decent human beings, all considered; and whether or not religion is still vital in our lives, most of us are ready to admit that Christianity, Canadian style, has contributed a good deal to that decency.

But no one could claim that 'the suffering of the church' has

19 trans. by R.A. Wilson and John Bowden; London: S.C.M. Press, Ltd., 1974; p. 1.

been a strong theme of that Christianity - a hallmark of our theology and our faith. On the contrary, such a theme can only be heard by us as a peculiar one - distasteful to many, strange to most.

All the same, it is this strange song that we are here and there *beginning* to learn, and that we shall have to become still more familiar with in the years ahead. We are beginning to learn it as we move from the predominantly anglo- and francophone societies that we have been to a country increasingly peopled by human beings of other ethnic, racial and religious backgrounds - refugees, many of them, from worlds of unending pain. We are beginning to hear this song as we listen to the minorities in our own midst whom we have oppressed - and oppressed, partly, because our national code of O.K.-ism precluded any overt expressions of dissatisfaction from those who were not O.K.

We are acquiring some rudimentary awareness of this theme, too, as we contemplate the (perhaps irreversible) damage that we have done to what we imagined an infinitely resillient natural order, and as we come out from underneath the umbrella of a world view which assumed that in every way, every day, we were getting better and better. The future we have begun (just begun!) to think about is full of frightening prospects that "they" - the architects of Modernity - never told us about. Now we hear wise and concerned commentators on the human condition telling us that "our grandchildren are going to live in a truly awful world no matter what we do at this point ..." - a strange song indeed for a people reared on the "religion of Progress" (George Grant); and it hardly cushions the sting of such statements, which are frequent, when their authors add, "... but it may not be too late to ensure that they at least live."[20]

In sum, we are beginning - as a people, not only as Christians - to realize that what we have had here in Canada, and still in some measurable degree have, is quite unusual: a place where the

[20] Gwynne Dyer, in *The Gazette*, Montreal, 16.7.88.

optimistic credo of the Modern era, while never so uncritically and enthusiastically trumpeted as in the United States, could seem basically right, at least for those who were 'making' our history. But now we ask - or fear to ask: Was it just a postponement?

Where are we headed? Personally, I do not pretend to know very much about what the future holds for us, either as Canadians or as Christians. I seriously doubt that it will be the "land of hope and glory" that we sang about in my village during the war. On the other hand, I am not ready to opine with Mr. Dyer that it *will be* "truly awful" - that this is just inevitable. Certainly he is right - and so are the many others - in telling us that all *the makings* of 'true awfulness' are present and accounted for in the "great instabilities" (Charles Birch) that are currently shaking the foundations of the whole civilization. But must we accept all these negating factors with "serenity," or can some of them "be changed?" As I insisted at the outset, biblical faith is not interested primarily in *predicting* the future but in *influencing* it. And so far as I have been given to understand these things, the only influence that matters comes from those, whoever they are, whose "wisdom" combines a high degree of honest realism with a determined protest against what is regularly perceived as realism.

So far as Christianity is concerned, realism is grounded in the recognition that existence under the conditions of history entails suffering. "Reality itself - not the abstract reality of physics, but the full-bodied reality of human life - is cruciform."[21] The cross that is at the centre of our faith reminds us that any who would enter deeply into the creaturely condition must be prepared to experience something of the agony and abandonment that Jesus underwent. There is no place in the community of serious discipleship today for the kind of 'positive thinking' that refuses even to admit that we are living in a dangerous world. To affect real change, it is necessary

---

[21] Eugen Rosenstock-Huessy, *The Christian Future: Or the Modern Mind Outrun* (New York: Harper and Row, 1946), p. 166.

to expose oneself to the forces which threaten and negate life - to enter at least the *environs* of Golgotha (Barth). Everything else is a half-way measure - 'healing the wounds of my people lightly.'

But the cross at the centre also reminds us that *God* has already entered into midst of our "cruciform" world, that *Light* has penetrated this darkness, and is not overcome by it. "We are not alone . . . ." And this is the source of our ongoing protest against "reality." There are possibilities even in the face of the impossible. There is hope even in the midst of despair. There is life even in the kingdom of death.

This much, therefore, we may conclude with *confidence*: the Church that is enabled to endure the suffering of those who follow Jesus Christ into earth's uncertain future will itself have a future. Willing to lose its life for his sake who lost his life for the world's sake, it will find its life. And however insignificant and inglorious that life may appear in comparison with all that our imperial Christian past has conditioned us to expect, it will be . . . *exceptional!*